THÉRÈSE RAQUIN

Based on the novel by Emile Zola

Adultery was the least of their crimes

Begins April 12   Sundays at 9 PM   Channel 13 PBS

Masterpiece Theatre

Mobil®

Design: Gips+Balkind+Associates Illustration: Chuck Wilkinson

Twenty Seasons of
Mobil Masterpiece Theatre
1971-1991

Editor: Gregory Vitiello
Designer: Derek Birdsall
Program notes by Gregory Vitiello
Production supervised by Martin Lee
Photographs courtesy of Frank & Arlene Goodman Associates
Photo research by Deborah Richardson
Listings compiled by Nathan Hasson
Printed in the United States by Acme Printing Co.,
Wilmington, Massachusetts

Contents

7   Foreword by Allen E. Murray

9   A Personal Memoir by Alistair Cooke

11   By Way of Homage: Brendan Gill

15   Jean Marsh Remembers . . .

18   The Season of 1971-72
24   The Season of 1972-73
30   The Season of 1973-74
34   The Season of 1974-75
38   The Season of 1975-76
42   The Season of 1976-77
46   The Season of 1977-78
52   The Season of 1978-79
58   The Season of 1979-80
64   The Season of 1980-81
70   The Season of 1981-82
76   The Season of 1982-83
80   The Season of 1983-84
84   The Season of 1984-85
88   The Season of 1985-86
92   The Season of 1986-87
96   The Season of 1987-88
100   The Season of 1988-89
104   The Season of 1989-90
108   The Season of 1990-91

112   Index
        Acknowledgements

Foreword

This book commemorates the 20th anniversary of Masterpiece Theatre. It is, in a sense, a celebration of the best that television has to offer – a shining example of what the medium is capable of doing, but seldom does.

Almost 10 years before Masterpiece Theatre premiered with "The First Churchills," then Federal Communications Commissioner Newton Minow assailed television as a "vast wasteland." Television's so-called golden age had ended with the demise of first-rate shows like Studio One and Playhouse 90. Public broadcasting was in its infancy, poised to fill the need for quality programming. It was in this environment that Masterpiece Theatre was born on January 10, 1971.

Looking back over 20 years, I'm sure each of us identifies with a favorite series or unforgettable performance. But what's equally memorable, I think, is this rich diversity of drama offered as Masterpiece Theatre evolved over the years. From costume dramas to adaptations of classic Victorian novels to the most contemporary images and issues, Masterpiece Theatre has kept its relevance and vitality by constant evolution. Side-by-side in the pages of this book – and week-after-week on the television screen – the timeless brilliance of Charles Dickens co-exists quite comfortably with an absorbing depiction of today's international drug cartel or a chillingly plausible account of what could come to pass in contemporary British politics.

Clearly, Masterpiece Theatre has changed over the years, though its commitment to quality has not. And Mobil's commitment to underwriting quality television has not only endured over the past two decades but broadened with the addition of the award-winning Mystery! series, now in its 11th year.

In the course of underwriting these programs, we've developed a special relationship with PBS stations throughout the country, whereby we've become partners in promoting Masterpiece Theatre and Mystery! to broader segments of the viewing public. We see our role as consistent with our belief in public broadcasting and its mission.

Much of the credit for this enduring quality of Masterpiece Theatre must go to WGBH, Boston's public television station, which, from the beginning, has selected and packaged the programs for broadcasting. And, certainly, special thanks go to Alistair Cooke, the series' urbane and inimitable host.

Most of all, we thank our viewers, who are the final arbiters of what comes into their living rooms each Sunday evening. Some of you have been with us over the years; many more have joined us of late. We know because we enjoy a constant dialogue with many of you.

So this book is dedicated to you – our viewers. Perhaps you first got hooked on "Upstairs, Downstairs." Or maybe it was "I, Claudius." Or "The Jewel in the Crown." No matter. The important thing is that Masterpiece Theatre, at age 20, is alive and well and living in the hearts and minds of millions of its fans.

I hope you enjoy this retrospective.

Allen E. Murray
Chairman and Chief Executive Officer
Mobil Corporation

MOBIL MASTERPIECE THEATRE PRESENTS

ON APPROVAL

EVERYONE DOES IT NOW—NO ONE DID IT THEN.

A SPECIAL TWO-HOUR PRESENTATION · STARRING JEREMY BRETT AND PENELOPE KEITH · SUNDAY MARCH 13 9PM CHANNEL 13 PBS

Mobil

Introduction by Alistair Cooke

In the first week of October, 1970, I was in Boston with a BBC television crew about to begin filming a documentary series that was intended to express my own historical view of the American experience from the Indian settlements to our own time. For over 30 years, my trade had been that of a foreign correspondent, reporting the United States to Britain and many foreign countries, and the BBC television moguls thought the time had come for me to have my say about America as Kenneth Clark had memorably had his say about "Civilisation."

"America" was much the most ambitious thing I had attempted on television, though I had been the host-writer of Robert Saudek's project, "Omnibus," a memorable weekly exercise in the arts and sciences that ran for nine years. "America," I had been warned, would absorb most of my working hours for two years or so of writing, traveling, filming, editing.

So when, on the morning of the 5th of October, 1970, I sat in a pew of the Old South Meeting House to memorize my first speech to camera, I already knew that nothing, no journalistic enterprise however beguiling, could possibly distract me from "America" or, for that matter, from "Letter From America," my weekly radio broadcast which, by then, the BBC had been transmitting for 25 years. I had reckoned without the intrusion of that legendary menace, a dark-haired stranger. Creeping, uninvited, into the Meeting House, came a young rogue of an Englishman, just as we took a break from filming the birth pangs of the American Revolution. He announced himself, in a deferential whisper, as one Christopher Sarson. He begged an urgent word with me about some program he was putting together for the Boston public television station. I told him that for the next two years there would be only one urgency in my life: it was the filming of the project he had rudely stumbled in on. Nevertheless, this patient – and I have to say persuasive – scamp went on quietly expounding his own project, which did, in fact, realize a fantasy that had lazed around at the back of my mind for some time. Namely, a weekly television theatre, composed of the best television adaptations of famous novels then being done not only by the BBC but by such independent producers as Granada and London Weekend. But Sarson was a year or more too late.

Could I not suggest some other appropriate writer, host-narrator, the role Sarson had imagined would be mine? I could and did, drolly putting forward the names of Max Beerbohm and Alexander Woolcott. (The Boston studio phoned me a week or two later to say they were both dead. So they were.) It must have been a month or more before the artful Sarson, feigning desperation, called me to say that his program had already acquired some very high-toned dramas, including adaptations of works by Tolstoy, Thackeray, Hardy, but the missing link was still the commentating host. Would I reconsider? He sounded so helpless, so bereft. He was so deeply sincere. Let me put it this way: I said yes. (I am told that Sarson has his own, discrepant, version of this meeting. It is false!)

So, during the next 18 months, I found myself flying in to Boston, for a snatched two-day "Masterpiece" stint, from remote or familiar locations across the United States. The preparatory routine has stayed the same for 20 years: get the videotapes from the United Kingdom; watch them and take notes; bone up on any necessary research; write and type out my intros – and extros; fly to Boston, appear in the studio, memorize the first intro, film it, shoo the crew away, learn the next intro, shoot it, and so on and on and on till day is done.

I have to admit now that my hopes for the longevity of Masterpiece Theatre were pretty dim after we had finished our first series: a very "busy," dressed-up costume melodrama, cluttered with troops of actors wearing important names (and, it appeared, identical black wigs), most of whom liked to stand with back to camera, thus making identification – as between heroes and extras – almost impossible. It was called "The First Churchills." It was not a masterpiece, acknowledged or unsung. It was not even a dramatized novel. It was a television original. Even so, the initiation of Masterpiece Theatre was received without derision or undue mirth. We passed quickly and noiselessly on to – in sequence – dramatizations of Henry James, Dostoyevsky, Balzac, Hardy, Tolstoy, and Stella Gibbons, pausing for a three-month bout of rattling costume drama ("The Six Wives of Henry VIII" and "Elizabeth R") before reverting to the Masterpiece stride. At the end of our second season, by January, 1973, we had at least established the propriety of calling ourselves "Masterpiece" Theatre. At best, we had introduced into American television the novelty of what came to be called the mini-series. And we had transmitted over the public television network many examples of fine television writing and acting such as were then rarely to be seen on our own commercial networks. We also acquired – thanks mainly to the Henry VIII and Elizabeth series – the label, not to say the stigma, of "costume drama," a classification that, to some irregular viewers, has stayed with us even after many years of plays about late 19th century life, about the First and Second World Wars, comedies and dramas of the years in between, and a couple of projections of British political and social life a year or two ahead of our time.

Our own prescriptive rule of choice – which is to say, the rule of our producers, Rebecca Eaton and the late Joan Wilson, who did the choosing – has always been the same: find the best work available, whether it was written by Jane Austen or Harold Pinter.

We know that to find 52 first-rate programs a year is an impossibility. (If Shakespeare had been a television dramatist, he would have been used up after a year or two.) I think my wife has it right about Masterpiece Theatre: "It may not always be up to scratch, but week in, week out, it's the best theatre in town."

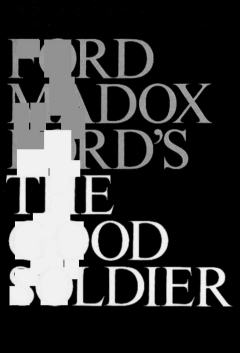

FORD MADOX FORD'S THE GOOD SOLDIER

A perfect gentleman and a perennial rake

With Masterpiece Theatre Favorites Jeremy Brett, Robin Ellis and Elizabeth Garvie

Mobil Masterpiece Theatre
A special two-hour presentation
Sunday January 9
9pm PBS

Mobil

By Way of Homage: Brendan Gill

Anniversaries smite us pell-mell. Moreover, as we grow older certain kinds of anniversaries – birthdays, school and college reunions, and the like – seem, defying nature, to circle round at ever-increasing speed. As individuals, we may feel no especially urgent sense of time passing, thanks to the fact that, in Henry James's phrase, "we are all young to life." (Even the corpulent, sedentary James in his late years sought with boyish glee to master that newly fashionable contraption, the bicycle.) Nevertheless, events that seem to repeat themselves at shorter and shorter intervals induce in us a certain degree of dread instead of anticipation. I recall a drawing that appeared in the "New Yorker" magazine, in which a husband, seated at his desk and with open checkbook in hand, looks up at his wife and says in evident alarm, "Christmas is at our throats again!" In a more welcome way, there are anniversaries that take us by surprise, seizing us not by the throat but by the hand and drawing us into the midst of unexpected festivities. The 20th birthday of Masterpiece Theatre is just such an occasion and we do well to celebrate it.

On first learning of this anniversary, I felt a sense of shock – tritely there leapt to mind the words, "How is it possible? Twenty years! Where has the time gone?" – followed by a surge of satisfaction at the success to which so long a span of existence on television eloquently attests. For in the world of entertainment as a whole and in the world of TV entertainment in particular 20 years has an enviable, Methusaleh-like ring to it, approaching the miraculous. As a somewhat wary TV watcher, I have been struck by the fact that Sophocles' harsh dictum – "Never to be born is best" – accurately predicts the fate of most TV programming. How many times have we observed infant programs being ushered onto the airwaves in the confident hope of enjoying a year or two of glory? Programs that have then abruptly succumbed to the dire big chill of inattention, the humiliating death of a thousand switched dials!

The long life of Masterpiece Theatre is all the more remarkable because of the dark suspicion voiced over the years by some critics (not without an undertone of sadistic relish) that TV by its nature is unlikely to find a place for works of dramatic art as ambitious in their intentions as those of Masterpiece Theatre. In their view, a program that sought not only to achieve lofty standards of excellence but also to attract an audience that would respect and encourage those standards was doomed to suffer an early demise. By the reckoning of these doomsayers, there simply weren't enough people – out of 240 million Americans! – to enjoy productions aimed at the highest common denominator instead of the lowest.

Some of the doomsayers had another and more jingoistic objection to make, namely that Masterpiece Theatre was engaged in ransacking the best of British television entertainment and fobbing it off on credulous American viewers. Not that these viewers were ever clearly identified. Sometimes they were said to be a group composed of highly educated, induratedly snobbish Anglophiles; at other times, they were said to consist of ignorant yokels humbly in awe of any manifestation of transatlantic culture that happened to reach our shores employing a tony Oxford accent. The obvious answer to the complaint that the program didn't originate in America was (and is) the good old American slang phrase, "So what?" Do we not honor excellence in any field of endeavor without regard to national boundaries? As for the audience that is capable of responding to excellence, should we assign customs inspectors to riffle through their luggage in search of contraband motives? (Speaking for myself, I am both an Anglophile *and* in some areas of knowledge – mathematics, physics, and similar topics – I am also an ignorant yokel.)

Fortunately, it has turned out that the doomsayers were wrong on all counts; Masterpiece Theatre has marched from strength to strength through the decades of the seventies and eighties, and its now ample archives bestow upon the hundreds of participants in the programs assurance of a place in the pantheon of television immortals. Among these participants are actors, writers, directors, and designers, to say nothing of the suave, blue-eyed, white-haired Grand Panjandrum himself, Alistair Cooke, cozily ensconced in a wing chair in the library of some imaginary English country house as he elucidates plots and illuminates characters with an unchallengeable aplomb.

I would add that if there is a pantheon reserved for loyal corporate sponsors, then the Mobil Corporation deserves a conspicuous niche in it. From the inaugural Masterpiece Theatre program of January 10th, 1971 – "The First Churchills," produced by the BBC and running for 12 weeks – Mobil has underwritten a total of 121 programs, taking care to accompany them with advertising posters that have become classic examples of how to furnish pertinent information in a context of superb graphic design. In recent years, people have striven to collect Mobil Masterpiece Theatre posters with an ardor usually reserved for the posters of Mucha and Toulouse-Lautrec.

The Masterpiece Theatre archives that I spoke of exist not only in order to preserve for historians of the future a full documentary record of the past; they exist also in order to be examined by those of us among the living who may wish to rekindle our memories of certain favorite productions. How lucky we are to have access to performances that, in an earlier age, would have been lost to us forever! To glance over a list of Masterpiece Theatre productions is, in a sense, to take the measure of a portion of our own lives – to dip into a scrapbook that we hadn't been conscious of our having kept. And so great is the influence of drama upon our imaginations that certain make-believe adventures and misadventures depicted on Masterpiece Theatre may prove more vivid in our memories than the actual adventures and misadventures that we were experiencing at the same moment and that have since vanished without a trace.

For the pleasure it gives me, let me summon up a few of the Masterpiece Theatre productions that have never lost their crotchety British freshness in my mind's eye and that sometimes prompt me in quite alien circumstances (riding a crowded New York City subway, flying late at night over the snowy Rockies) to recollect a particular comic scene with such delight that I break out laughing, to the bewilderment of my fellow passengers. The scene may have drifted into my consciousness from Dorothy L. Sayers' "Murder Must Advertise," broadcast back in 1974 and starring Ian Carmichael as the nobleman-detective Lord Peter Wimsey, or it may have emerged from the whirligig of Somerville and Ross's "The Real Charlotte," broadcast only last spring. Other scenes that I cherish I plucked long ago from such novels as Stella Gibbons' *Cold Comfort Farm*, Somerset Maugham's *Cakes and Ale*, and Aldous Huxley's *Point Counterpoint*, and from *I, Claudius*, the fictional biography of a Roman Emperor, written by Robert Graves, adapted by Jack Pulman, and starring Derek Jacobi and John Hurt.

Novels that are internationally acknowledged to be at the pinnacle of literary merit – Flaubert's *Madame Bovary*, Hardy's *Jude the Obscure*, Tolstoy's *Anna Karenina*, and James's *The Golden Bowl* – have been adapted for television by writers as adroit in their craft as they are fearless in the taking of risks. (A great work of fiction resists being tampered with in the course of being transformed into successful theatre; if on a stage actions nearly always speak louder than words, in a novel words are permitted to speak louder than actions.) Many of the dramatized novels on Masterpiece Theatre are serialized over several weeks, as in the 19th century the novels of Dickens and other popular writers were serialized in magazines; the suspense generated by the plot of a novel is much heightened by our being obliged to follow its unfolding at a pace that no impatience on our part can hope to quicken.

This winter, as part of its 20th anniversary celebration, Masterpiece Theatre is offering a nine-week-long sampler of a number of its most distinguished programs, including episodes from "Upstairs, Downstairs," "The Jewel in the Crown," and "The Six Wives of Henry VIII." Which is to say that, in the admirable tradition of all birthday celebrations, we in the audience will perform the Janus-feat of simultaneously looking backward and forward, and in both directions with equal gratitude.

Masterpiece Theatre
presents
the final, 'Roaring 20s' season
of

Upstairs, Downstairs

Winner of six Emmy awards
Host: Alistair Cooke
16 New Episodes beginning January 16
Sunday Evenings on Channel 13 PBS

Mobil

CHERMAYEFF & GEISMAR ASSOCIATES

Jean Marsh remembers...

What I remember, first of all, was the fizzy excitement I felt when John Whitney, the producer to whom I'd taken the idea for "Upstairs, Downstairs," said: "It's a wonderful idea. We'd like to do it."

The fizzy excitement that day was helped by the champagne I drank over lunch in a rather posh restaurant. But I remember another day when I didn't feel so fizzy. Eileen Atkins, my co-creator, and I were asked who should write the series. And since we didn't know any television writers, we naïvely suggested Harold Pinter. Eventually, of course, we got to work with quite a few television writers as well as wonderful novelists like Elizabeth Jane Howard and Fay Weldon.

My next strong memory is of the first rehearsal. Looking around the table (on which one of the actors later carved the words, "This table was based on an idea by Jean Marsh"), I thought everybody *looked* so right, but would they sound right? About 20 minutes into that first read-through, I knew that something important was happening: They sounded right – better than right – and everything worked. We could have filmed the first episode that afternoon.

I especially noted the faces of Evin Crowley, an Irish actress, the "tweeny," lowest of the low in the servants' hall, and George Innes, the footman. Evin's face sometimes looked Dickensian in its gawky plainness, but it could also transform itself into simple beauty. And George, an original and daring actor, made his odd but attractive face into a mask of reluctant servility. Those two actors were so good they had special episodes written for them; sadly, these episodes meant they left the series after Evin's character died and George's was disgraced. Since nobody anticipated how long the series would run, none of the actors had a contract beyond the current series.

Everybody in the cast had a different way of learning lines. Gordon Jackson spent long evenings at home working on his lines. Angela Baddeley also learned her lines at home, and on the first day of rehearsal, knew them all. But gradually she forgot them all and had to start over again. The rest of us learned most of our lines at home and completed the process at rehearsals. In fact, learning them perfectly made it more difficult to adjust whenever lines were changed, rewritten, or cut.

Our growing familiarity with each other and our roles made rehearsals easier and faster but sometimes made our performances superficial. That was where directors were invaluable, stopping you from becoming facile. One of my favorite directors, Raymond Menmuir, was ruthless in his hatred of sentimentality and his demand for honest work. I think the most complimentary thing he ever said to me was, "O.K., that was all right. Do it again."

I used my mother's Cockney dialect so that Rose's accent would be authentic, but I had to be aware that authenticity was only commendable if the audience understood the words.

Also, because of my nearsightedness, I couldn't see the man cueing me for an entrance. I eventually got my cues by having a red flag waved off camera (as long as it didn't disturb the other actors) or by being prodded from behind by a long pole.

For each episode, we had eight days' rehearsal out of the studio, followed by a day in the studio for setting up, and a day for taping. Since taping was pressure-filled, we always used the first day in the studio to let off steam by playing with our costumes and wigs, teasing each other, and engaging in other frivolity. Sometimes this playfulness helped us to gain insights into our characters, which we incorporated into our performances on the next day.

Only Gordon, who was an anxious man, was spared from our teasing. But I remember the day he shook with laughter when he had to say Grace before lunch in the servants' hall. Lunch consisted of gristly-looking bits of an unidentifiable animal floating in a sea of gray oil with lumps of congealed fat nestling in it. Gordon was trying to say, "Oh Lord, for Thy gracious bounty, we thank Thee," but he barely managed it.

Our rehearsal rooms were located all over London, mainly in Boys Clubs in varying degrees of uncleanliness. We ended up in our favorite, a huge hall in an army barracks in the Kings Road, Chelsea. Its only drawback was mice. They were calm, almost tame creatures. One sat on the director's desk while he worked on camera scripts; since he was from the country, the mouse didn't bother him. Finally, we got an official army cat, a large tabby, which we called Sergeant Major Pussy Cat. But even though Sergeant Major Pussy Cat killed all the mice, he didn't dispose of them or eat them; instead, he saved them for later. We found their little bodies everywhere: in a saucepan, among the downstairs props, in an old shoe, in an orange box used as Mrs. Bridges' sink, and – since the cat was no respecter of class – under a cushion on Lady Marjorie's favorite chair.

Rachel Gurney, as Lady Marjorie, was one of several cast members with whom I became close friends. A great beauty, with fine bone structure, she had an air of authority, an upper-class confidence that was a little intimidating but was absolutely right for Lady Marjorie. In fact, as I learned, her looks belied her character, for she was really a hesitant, gentle, slightly insecure person in need of approval and encouragement.

Equally, Pauline Collins' appearance was deceptive. A pretty, cuddly girl with large round eyes and a puppyish enthusiasm, she turned out to be a practical woman with a formidable intelligence. And then there were my favorites, Angela and Gordon, sadly both dead now.

Angela, or Miss Baddeley as I first called her, became my first "Upstairs, Downstairs" friend. I was of the age that still used last names out of respect for those who were older, more famous, or more successful, and Angela liked that respect. She was one of the funniest and naughtiest actors I've ever worked with. During a recording, she sometimes tried to make me laugh by raising an eyebrow to comment on another actor's work. Sometimes when we sat watching rehearsals, we held hands, while her sweet, seemingly placid face masked her devastating comments on what was going on. But somehow it was never bitchy, and she was a very shrewd judge of acting and character.

And then there was Gordon. He was loved by all of us, especially me. Ever since he died in early 1990, the pain of missing him has been with me every day – and there's so much to miss. He was a complicated man, full of enthusiasms and full of doubt about his enormous talent. The calm authority he showed as Mr. Hudson came from hours of work. Because he had to spend so much time alone with his script, he always said he was a boring husband. But his beautiful wife Rona, herself an actress, understood his needs well and I doubt she found him at all boring. Nor did anyone else.

He was a great authority on classical music and played the piano very well. Dinner at the Jacksons' usually ended with Gordon at the piano and the guests singing along. Whenever I hummed a phrase of something I'd heard on the radio, he immediately identified it and told me who made the best recording of it, and often arrived the next day with the record.

One of the best and warmest things about him was his kindness to his fellow actors. After a few seasons of "Upstairs, Downstairs" we had become a close-knit group. But Gordon was always aware of how intimidating that closeness could be to new cast members, and he made it his business to make them feel at home. This wasn't just sympathy; he had a real interest in everybody.

He was fascinated by my clothes, which I suppose were a bit eccentric. His favorites were my long white Indian shift embroidered with tiny mirrors, and a large shirt made from flour sacks. He questioned me about them so he could describe them to Rona. Once, after I'd been playing poor, plain Rose for a couple of years, he reproached me for letting the part affect my private wardrobe. He said that half the fun of rehearsals was seeing what I wore, but now I was becoming too conventional.

He was a man of strong contrasts, who took pains to produce his work and yet was full of *joie de vivre*. He made other people feel interesting. My strongest memory is of him saying, "Och, you're marvelous," but it was Gordon Jackson who was marvelous.

All of us in the production were amazed and thrilled when the series was sold to American television. But why Masterpiece Theatre? Surely we weren't a masterpiece? Well, if Americans said so, so be it! At the completion of the first series, Mobil and PBS brought me to America for five weeks to publicize "Upstairs, Downstairs." Before I set off, nearly every member of the cast gave me a good-luck gift. They ranged from books from Gordon to vitamins from David Langton (Mr. Bellamy). They were all pleased for me, and if they were envious, they never showed it.

By the time the series was in its second season, we all had to guard against thinking we knew better than the writers. In truth, sometimes we did – but not always. On at least one occasion, each of us said, "Ruby (or Lady Marjorie) wouldn't say that," and even, among those who closely identified with their character, "*I* wouldn't say that."

During the five years of "Upstairs, Downstairs," we experienced all the usual small and great things that happen to people. Babies were born, relationships broke up, teeth were capped, hair went gray, weight was put on and lost, houses were bought.

And in the years since? Most of the cast have worked successfully: David Langton appearing in London's West End; Christopher Beeny in a half-hour sit-com; Pauline Collins playing the title role in "Shirley Valentine" to universal acclaim; Nicola Pagett starring in "The Rehearsal" in London. Meg Wynn Owen has not only acted but become a successful landscape gardener. Simon Williams has acted and produced, and has written a best-selling thriller. And me? I spend my time in New York, where I've been in two Broadway plays, and in an isolated rural retreat in England. Simon and his wife live nearby on a farm and he often walks over to visit and give me advice about the garden and the chickens.

When I walk the seven miles to visit him, he insists on cleaning my muddy hiking boots. I sit in the large, warm farmhouse kitchen with a marmalade cat on my lap and see not Simon but Master James, and I wonder, what would Rose think?

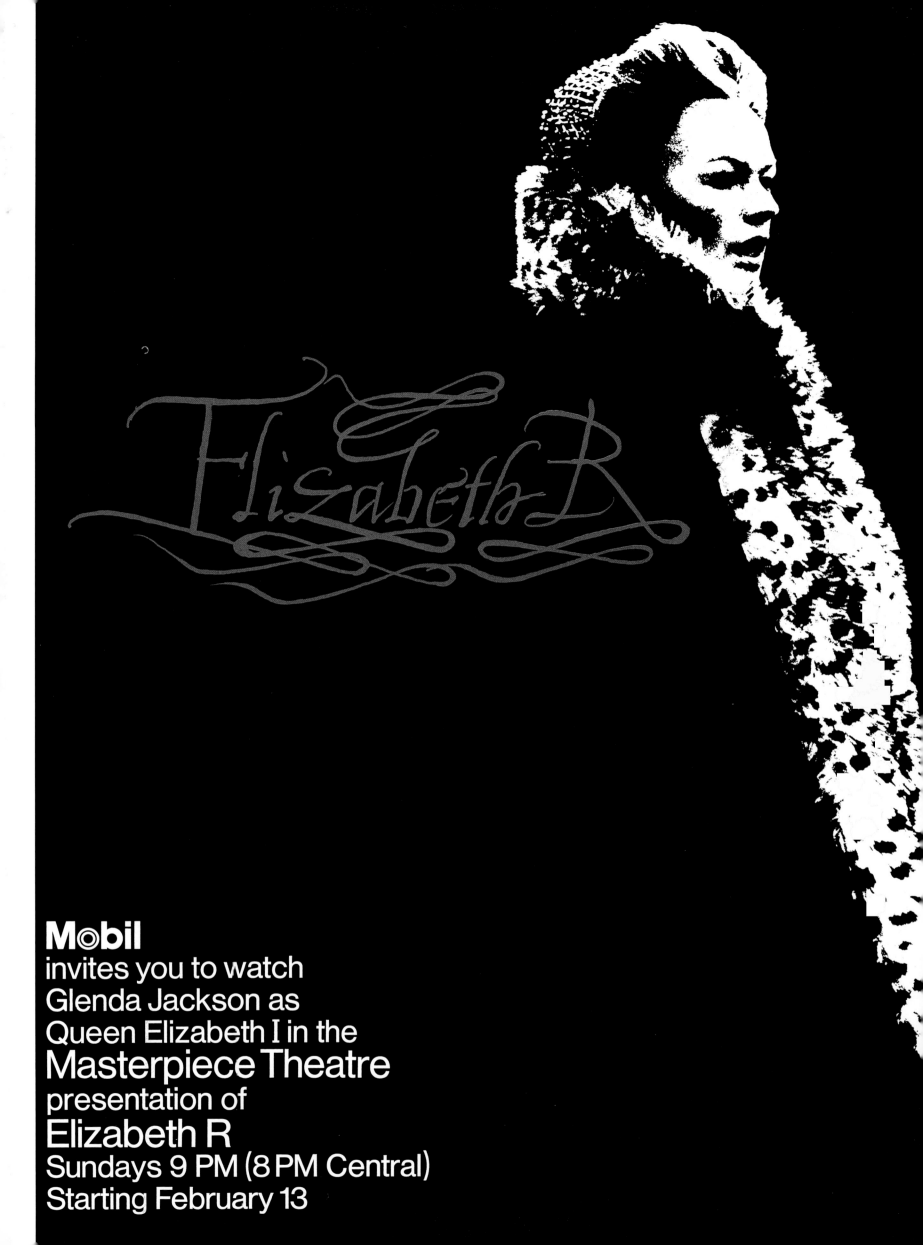

M⊙bil
invites you to watch
Glenda Jackson as
Queen Elizabeth I in the
Masterpiece Theatre
presentation of
Elizabeth R
Sundays 9 PM (8 PM Central)
Starting February 13

THE FIRST CHURCHILLS
(12 episodes)

January 10 – March 28, 1971
Repeat: July 11 – September 26, 1971

Produced by: BBC
Original story by Donald Wilson
Dramatized by: Donald Wilson
Producer: Donald Wilson
Director: David Giles
Music: Arrangements by Marcus Dods

Starring: Susan Hampshire, John Neville, James Villiers, John Standing & Margaret Tyzack

1970/71
Emmy Award: Best Actress:
Susan Hampshire,
THE FIRST CHURCHILLS

THE SPOILS OF POYNTON
(4 episodes)

April 4 – April 25, 1971
Repeat: July 9 – July 30, 1972

Produced by: BBC
Based on the novel by Henry James
Dramatized by: Denis Constanduros
Producer: Martin Lisemore
Director: Peter Sasdy

Starring: Ian Ogilvy, Gemma Jones, Diane Fletcher & Pauline Jameson

THE POSSESSED
(6 episodes)

May 2 – June 6, 1971
Repeat: May 21 – June 25, 1972

Produced by: BBC
Based on the novel by Fyodor Dostoyevsky
Dramatized by: Hugh Leonard
Producer: David Conroy
Director: Naomi Capon

Starring: Rosalie Crutchley, Keith Bell, Joan Hickson & Joseph O'Conor

PERE GORIOT
(4 episodes)

June 13 – July 4, 1971
Repeat: June 14 – July 15, 1973

Produced by: BBC
Based on the novel by Honoré de Balzac
Dramatized by: David Turner
Producer: David Conroy
Director: Paddy Russell

Starring: Michael Goodliffe, Angela Browne, Andrew Keir, Anna Cropper & Moira Redmond

JUDE THE OBSCURE
(6 episodes)

October 3 – November 7, 1971

Produced by: BBC
Based on the novel by Thomas Hardy
Dramatized by: Harry Green
Producer: Martin Lisemore
Director: Hugh David

Starring: Robert Powell, Fiona Walker, Alex Marshall & John Franklyn-Robbins

THE GAMBLER
(2 episodes)

November 14 – November 21, 1971
Repeat: June 10 – June 17, 1973

Produced by: BBC
Based on the novel by Fyodor Dostoyevsky
Dramatized by: John Hopkins
Producer: David Conroy
Director: Michael Ferguson

Starring: Dame Edith Evans, Colin Redgrave, Maurice Roëves, Philip Madoc & John Phillips

RESURRECTION
(4 episodes)

November 28 – December 19, 1971

Produced by: BBC
Based on the novel by Leo Tolstoy
Dramatized by: Alexander Baron
Script Editor: Lennox Phillips
Producer: David Conroy
Director: David Giles

Starring: Alan Dobie, Brian Murphy, Tina Mathews & Bridget Turner

COLD COMFORT FARM
(1 episode)

December 6, 1971
Repeat: July 2, 1972

Produced by: BBC
Based on the novel by Stella Gibbons
Dramatized by: David Turner
Producer: David Conroy
Director: Peter Hammond

Starring: Rosalie Crutchley, Peter Egan, Alastair Sim, Freddie Jones, Brian Blessed, Fay Compton & Sarah Badel

THE SIX WIVES OF HENRY VIII
(6 episodes, 90 minutes each)

January 1 – February 6, 1972

Produced by: BBC
Based on an idea by Maurice Cowan
Producers: Mark Shivas and Ronald Travers
Music arranged by David Munrow

Starring: Keith Michell as Henry VIII

"Catherine of Aragon"
Dramatized by: Rosemary Anne Sisson
Director: John Glenister
Starring: Annette Crosbie

"Anne Boleyn"
Original drama by: Nick McCarty
Director: Naomi Capon
Starring: Dorothy Tutin

"Jane Seymour"
Original drama by: Ian Thorne
Director: John Glenister
Starring: Anne Stallybrass

"Anne of Cleves"
Original drama by: Jean Morris
Director: John Glenister
Starring: Elvi Hale

"Catherine Howard"
Original drama by: Beverley Cross
Director: Naomi Capon
Starring: Angela Pleasence

"Catherine Parr"
Original drama by: John Prebble
Director: Naomi Capon
Starring: Rosalie Crutchley

1971/72
Emmy Award:
Outstanding Single Performance in a
Leading Role:
Keith Michell, THE SIX WIVES OF
HENRY VIII

ELIZABETH R
(6 episodes, 90 minutes each)

February 13 – March 19, 1972

Produced by: BBC
Producer: Roderick Graham
Starring: Glenda Jackson as Queen Elizabeth I
With: Rosalie Crutchley, Robin Ellis, Robert
Hardy, Peter Jeffrey & Vivian Pickles

"The Lion's Cub"
Original drama by: John Hale
Director: Claude Whatham

"The Marriage Game"
Original drama by: Rosemary Anne Sisson
Director: Herbert Wise

"Shadow in the Sun"
Original drama by: Julian Mitchell
Director: Richard Martin

"Horrible Conspiracies"
Original drama by: Hugh Whitemore
Director: Roderick Graham

"Enterprise of England"
Original drama by: John Prebble
Director: Donald McWhinnie

"Sweet England's Pride"
Original drama by: Ian Rodger
Director: Roderick Graham

1971/72
Emmy Awards:
Outstanding Single Performance in a
Leading Role:
Glenda Jackson, ELIZABETH R
Outstanding Continued Performance in a
Leading Role in a Dramatic Series:
Glenda Jackson, ELIZABETH R
Outstanding Achievement in Costume Design:
Elizabeth Waller, ELIZABETH R
Outstanding New Series:
ELIZABETH R
Outstanding Drama Series:
ELIZABETH R

THE LAST OF THE MOHICANS
(8 episodes)

March 26 – May 14, 1972
Repeat: August 6 – September 24, 1972

Produced by: BBC
Based on the novel by:
James Fenimore Cooper
Dramatized by: Harry Green
Producer: John McRae
Director: David Maloney

Starring: Philip Madoc, Joanna David,
Richard Warwick, John Abineri & Tim
Goodman

Elizabeth R

Just as Henry VIII dominates the first six episodes of the BBC's 12-part Tudor cycle, so his daughter, Queen Elizabeth I, dominates the other six.

"Elizabeth R" begins with Henry's death in 1547 and ends 56 years later with the death of Elizabeth.

For Elizabeth, the way to the throne is tortuous, for she is third in line behind her half-brother Edward and her half-sister Mary. Both her siblings rule briefly, and both die, but only after the Roman Catholic Mary has banished the Protestant Elizabeth to the Tower of London.

This imprisonment caps an unhappy youth for Elizabeth. Her father ignored her because he wanted a son. Her mother and stepmother were beheaded. And her life has been threatened by Mary's campaign to abolish the Church of England in favor of Catholicism.

Elizabeth's accession to the throne in 1558 is welcomed with rejoicing by a people whose nation is almost bankrupted by wars and buffeted by political and religious tensions.

Elizabeth proves worthy of their optimism. She combines, says Alistair Cooke, "intellectual power, secretiveness, generosity, stinginess, a peasant shrewdness, courage, deviousness, tenderness, inflexibility, authority softened by irony, vanity tempered by self-knowledge."

This complex woman has been played by many actresses. "In this television series," Cooke says, "Glenda Jackson, playing with spunkiness, intelligence, and an engaging guile, has nothing to fear from her predecessors."

"Elizabeth R" depicts a queen who is prudent in her choice of advisers, but trusts none of them exclusively. She is equally prudent with her suitors. To marry a French or Spanish nobleman might save her country from war. But for Elizabeth, the price – surrendering either to Catholicism or to the lesser status of a consort – is too great. So she remains single.

As queen, she is tolerant of her Catholic citizens – including her cousin, Mary, Queen of Scots. But after Mary plots to kill Elizabeth and usurp her throne, the Queen signs the warrant for Mary's execution.

Ever an effective ruler, Elizabeth wards off England's greatest challenge when her navy defeats the Spanish Armada. "With the defeat of the Armada," Cooke says, "the legendary Elizabethan Age began."

But for Elizabeth, and the series, there is one final episode: old age. She tries to hide its incursion by wearing a permanent mask, "a lotion made of white of egg, powdered eggshell, alum borax, and poppy seeds mixed with mill water."

Even so, she has one last romance with the young, ambitious Earl of Essex. But after he leads a rebellion against her, she orders his execution.

The series ends with her death at the age of 70.

Glenda Jackson, as Princess Elizabeth, at the Tower of London.

The life of "Elizabeth R" spans more than half a century, from the years after her father Henry's death (right) through her long reign (below, with Ronald Hines as Lord Burghley).

The Six Wives of Henry VIII

The year is 1509. The 18-year-old king, Henry VIII, is madly in love with his first wife, Catherine of Aragon. By marrying her, he has allied himself with powerful Spain, reducing the immediate threat to Britain's autonomy. Even more urgent is his desire for a male heir who will preserve the Tudor dynasty founded by his father, Henry VII.

So begins "The Six Wives of Henry VIII." Each of its six episodes depicts one of Henry's marriages; each is written by a different author. All six bring to life, with accuracy and splendor, the intrigue, romance, and regalia of Henry's 38-year reign.

The series also reinforces Henry's place in history. "He left a deeper mark on the mind, heart and face of England than any event in English history between the coming of the Normans and the coming of the factories," wrote British historian J. J. Scarisbrick.

The seminal event in Henry's reign occurs when he decides to divorce Catherine for failing to produce a son. When the Pope opposes his plan to annul the marriage, Henry breaks with the Church of Rome and establishes a national Church owing allegiance only to him.

Henry's action leads to England's Protestant Reformation and its first national unity. In fact, his popularity endures for much of his reign, despite wars and Henry's cruel excesses.

Anne Boleyn, Henry's second wife, does bear a daughter, the future Queen Elizabeth I. But when she bears a still-born son, he turns against her – and has her executed on questionable charges of adultery and incest.

His only son, Edward, is the child of his marriage to Jane Seymour. Though he loves her, perhaps most of all his wives, he forces her to attend the christening in her weakened state, and she dies the same day.

His fourth marriage, to Anne of Cleves, is strictly expedient. She is a German princess, and Henry wants to reduce the threat from France and other continental enemies by forging an alliance with Protestant Germany. But once it becomes clear that France no longer threatens England, he divorces Anne on friendly terms.

Henry then marries Catherine Howard, a plump, foolish teenager whose uncle, the Duke of Norfolk, has sworn to her virginity. Rumors about her behavior, before and during her marriage, make her virginity doubtful. And when her uncle tells Henry she has been having extramarital affairs, the king has her beheaded along with two of her lovers.

Elegant, twice-widowed Catherine Parr is Henry's last wife. She becomes the nurse and companion of his final years – and the stepmother of his children.

Angela Pleasence as Catherine Howard,
Henry's fifth wife.

Keith Michell as Henry VIII, right, and below with Elvi Hale as Anne of Cleves.

VANITY FAIR
(5 episodes)

October 1 – October 29, 1972
Repeat: May 6 – June 3, 1973

Produced by: BBC
Based on the novel by:
William Makepeace Thackeray
Dramatized by: Rex Tucker
Producer: David Conroy
Director: David Giles

Starring: Susan Hampshire, Roy Marsden,
Richard Caldicott, Bryan Marshall & John
Moffatt

1972/73
Emmy Award:
Outstanding Continued Performance in a
Leading Role – Drama/Comedy Within a
Limited Series:
Susan Hampshire, VANITY FAIR

COUSIN BETTE
(5 episodes)

November 5 – December 3, 1972
Repeat: July 22 – August 19, 1973
Repeat: June 14 – July 12, 1981

Produced by: BBC
Based on the novel by Honoré de Balzac
Dramatized by: Ray Lawler
Producer: Martin Lisemore
Director: Gareth Davies

Starring: Margaret Tyzack, Helen Mirren,
Thorley Walters, Ursula Howells & Esmond
Knight

THE MOONSTONE
(5 episodes)

December 10, 1972 – January 7, 1973

Produced by: BBC
Based on the novel by Wilkie Collins
Dramatized by: Hugh Leonard
Producer: John McRae
Director: Paddy Russell

Starring: Colin Baker, Anna Cropper, Robin
Ellis, John Welsh & Martin Jarvis

TOM BROWN'S SCHOOLDAYS
(5 episodes)

January 14 – February 11, 1973

Produced by: BBC
Based on the novel by Thomas Hughes
Dramatized by: Anthony Steven
Producer: John McRae
Director: Gareth Davies

Starring: Iain Cuthbertson, Richard Morant
& Anthony Murphy

1972/73
Emmy Awards: Outstanding Drama/
Comedy Within a Limited Series:
TOM BROWN'S SCHOOLDAYS
Outstanding Continued Performance in a
Leading Role:
Anthony Murphy, TOM BROWN'S
SCHOOLDAYS

POINT COUNTERPOINT
(5 episodes)

February 18 – March 18, 1973

Produced by: BBC
Based on the novel by Aldous Huxley
Dramatized by: Simon Raven
Producer: David Conroy
Director: Rex Tucker

Starring: Sheila Grant & Max Adrian

THE GOLDEN BOWL
(6 episodes)

March 25 – April 29, 1973
Repeat: August 26 – September 30, 1973
Repeat: May 3 – June 12, 1981

Produced by: BBC
Based on the novel by Henry James
Dramatized by: Jack Pulman
Producer: Martin Lisemore
Director: James Cellan Jones
Music: Ravel's Introduction and Allegro

Starring: Gayle Hunnicutt, Daniel Massey,
Jill Townsend, Barry Morse & Cyril Cusack

Mobil Masterpiece Theatre Festival of Favorites
Henry James' **The Golden Bowl**

Two marriages too close for comfort
A six-part television series, PBS
Sundays at 9pm beginning May 3

Mobil

Cousin Bette

No writer was more prolific, or knew more about the society he satirized. Before he died at 50, Honoré de Balzac wrote 91 novels collected under the title *The Human Comedy*. In the last of them, *Cousin Bette*, he excoriated the greed and hypocrisy rampant in Paris in the middle of the 19th century.

Describing this world as "a snake pit with social trappings," Alistair Cooke says, "Balzac knew how society ticked from top to bottom, from the king to the pauper. He knew where power lay, far better than the politicians. He knew the movement of money better than the bankers. He showed a whole social population moved by what he observed as the fundamental drives – money, power, flattery, grand ambition."

Cousin Bette is a poor spinster, patronized by her wealthy, status-conscious family. Out of sheer generosity, she has befriended – and supported – a struggling young sculptor named Steinbock. But when he is lured away by her cousin Hortense, Bette plots her revenge against the entire family. By playing on their appetites for power and sex, she exposes them to each other.

In this BBC production, Cousin Bette is played by Margaret Tyzack, who portrayed Antonia in "I, Claudius" and won the British Oscar/Emmy as Queen Anne in "The First Churchills."

"*Cousin Bette* is the most ruthless of his 91 novels of devastating social satire," says Cooke. "It compressed in an agonizing combination all his vast and bitter knowledge of the world, and his still flickering belief in human goodness."

Balzac learned some of his hardest lessons at his father's knee. The family roots were modest, and when Balzac chose to be a writer, his father set him up in a Paris garret with a meager allowance – and waited for him to fail. Balzac vacillated – and even dreamed of becoming a tycoon – but he persevered. And he became his age's most incisive chronicler of its manners and morals.

Margaret Tyzack as Cousin Bette.

Right: Margaret Tyzack with Helen Mirren as Valerie.

Below: Tyzack with Esmond Knight as General Hulot and John Bryans as Grevel.

The Golden Bowl

A great miniaturist, Henry James wrote novels that prefigure Masterpiece Theatre: immaculately observed in physical detail and psychological nuance, unfolding gradually from one episode to another.

This subtlety – and underlying drama – is most impressive in *The Golden Bowl*, which James called his best and richest novel. Like much of James's work, it juxtaposes American innocence and European sophistication. Its four characters are Adam Verver, an American billionaire living in England; his adored daughter Maggie; Prince Amerigo, a descendant of explorer Amerigo Vespucci; and Charlotte Stant, Maggie's friend and the Prince's former lover.

Maggie marries the Prince, not knowing of his affair with Charlotte – which will soon resume. She then encourages her father's marriage to Charlotte, which further enmeshes the four characters.

Early in the story, Charlotte is shopping for a wedding present for Maggie and finds a golden bowl in an antique shop. The Prince discourages her from buying it because it is cracked – and is really just gilt crystal (a symbol for Maggie's flawed marriage). Maggie subsequently buys the bowl as a present for her father, and learns through the antique dealer's remarks of her husband's infidelity with Charlotte.

Critic Alfred Kazin writes that *The Golden Bowl* is "one of the most dramatic, suspense-laden, constantly absorbing and psychologically exciting novels in the world. What makes it so fascinating (in its own way as hypnotic as each member of this quadrille is to the other three) is the basic ferocity of the psychological drama in contrast with the sumptuousness, luxuriousness, and 'nobility' of the characters."

James, says his biographer Leon Edel, "wrote about the American tycoons as if they were Shakespeare's kings and queens." Their common dilemma is one of moral choices. Maggie, for example, is "a study of America's role in the civilized world . . . James's answer is that America must shed its naïvete and realize that civilization demands rules and standards – even elaborate myths – in order to make life possible."

"The success of this televised version," wrote Rosemary Say of London's *Sunday Telegraph*, "rests with the graciousness of the setting and the authentic musty atmosphere engendered by great wealth at the mercy of snobbery. The oft-repeated theme emerges slowly as the brash new world collides with impoverished European gentility."

Cyril Cusack as Bob Assingham.

Daniel Massey plays Prince Amerigo, an impoverished Italian aristocrat who loves Charlotte Stant (below, played by Gayle Hunnicutt) and marries Maggie Verver (right, played by Jill Townsend).

THE UNPLEASANTNESS AT THE BELLONA CLUB
(4 episodes)

December 2 – December 23, 1973
Repeat: September 8 – September 29, 1974

Produced by: BBC
Based on the novel by Dorothy L. Sayers
Dramatized by: John Bowen
Producer: Richard Beynon
Director: Ronald Wilson
Music: Herbert Chappell

Starring: Ian Carmichael, John Quentin,
Anna Cropper & Terence Alexander

THE LITTLE FARM
(1 episode)

December 30, 1973

Produced by: Granada Television
Based upon the story by H. E. Bates
Dramatized by: Hugh Leonard
Producer: Derek Granger
Director: Silvio Narizzano

Starring: Michael Elphick, Barbara Ewing,
Diane Keen & Bryan Marshall

UPSTAIRS, DOWNSTAIRS, Series I
(13 episodes)

January 6 – March 31, 1974
Repeat: April 7 – June 30, 1974

Produced by: London Weekend Television
Producer: John Hawkesworth

Starring: Jean Marsh, Gordon Jackson,
Angela Baddeley, David Langton, Rachel
Gurney, Simon Williams, Nicola Pagett &
Pauline Collins

"On Trial"
Original drama by: Fay Weldon
Director: Raymond Menmuir

"A Voice from the Past"
Original drama by: Jeremy Paul
Director: Raymond Menmuir

"For Love of Love"
Original drama by: Rosemary Anne Sisson
Director: Herbert Wise

"The New Man"
Original drama by: Rosemary Anne Sisson
Director: Raymond Menmuir

"A Pair of Exiles"
Original drama by: Alfred Shaughnessy
Director: Cyril Coke

"Whom God Hath Joined"
Original drama by: Jeremy Paul
Director: Bill Bain

"Guest of Honour"
Original drama by: Alfred Shaughnessy
Director: Bill Bain

"Out of the Everywhere"
Original drama by: Terence Brady and
Charlotte Bingham
Director: Christopher Hodson

"Object of Value"
Original drama by: Jeremy Paul
Director: Raymond Menmuir

"A Special Mischief"
Original drama by: Anthony Skene
Director: Raymond Menmuir

"The Fruits of Love"
Original drama by: John Hawkesworth
Director: Christopher Hodson

"The Wages of Sin"
Original drama by: Anthony Skene
Director: Christopher Hodson

"A Family Gathering"
Original drama by: Alfred Shaughnessy
Director: Raymond Menmuir

1973/74
Emmy Award: Outstanding Drama Series:
UPSTAIRS, DOWNSTAIRS

THE EDWARDIANS
(4 episodes)

July 7 – July 28, 1974

Produced by: BBC
Producer: Mark Shivas

"Lloyd George"
Dramatized by: Keith Dewhurst
Director: John Davies
Starring: Anthony Hopkins

"The Reluctant Juggler"
Dramatized by: Alan Plater
Director: Brian Farnham
Starring: Georgia Brown

"Mr Rolls and Mr Royce"
Dramatized by: Ian Curteis
Director: Gerald Blake
Starring: Robert Powell & Michael Jayston

"Conan Doyle"
Dramatized by: Jeremy Paul
Director: Brian Farnham
Starring: Nigel Davenport

CLOUDS OF WITNESS
(5 episodes)

October 7 – November 4, 1973
Repeat: August 4 – September 1, 1974

Produced by: BBC
Based on the novel by Dorothy L. Sayers
Dramatized by: Anthony Steven
Producer: Richard Beynon
Director: Hugh David

Starring: Ian Carmichael, Rachel Herbert,
David Langton & Mark Eden

THE MAN WHO WAS HUNTING HIMSELF
(3 episodes)

November 11 – November 26, 1973

Produced by: BBC
Original drama by: N. J. Crisp
Producer: Bill Sellers
Director: Terence Williams

Starring: Donald Burton, Carol Austin, David
Savile, Garfield Morgan & Lois Baxter

"Too good to miss"
John J. O'Connor, New York Times

Upstairs Downstairs

Sundays · 9pm

Channel 13

Masterpiece Theatre

made possible by a grant from

M⊙bil

Upstairs, Downstairs (Part I)

January 6, 1974, was a momentous date for public television and for Masterpiece Theatre. That night, viewers were taken inside 165 Eaton Place in the Belgravia section of London to meet the "Upstairs" Bellamys and their "Downstairs" servants.

What distinguished this night, and the ensuing four years of "Upstairs, Downstairs" on Masterpiece Theatre, was this rounded portrait of an upper-class British household and its help. What emerged was an entire social structure from Edwardian England in 1903 to the Crash in November, 1929.

What also emerged was public television's biggest hit, loved by viewers, applauded by critics, and festooned with awards, winning nine Emmys in four seasons.

It not only popularized the mini-series on American television but gave respectability to the term "soap opera." But it was more than a soap opera: ". . . if Masterpiece Theatre can claim to have exhibited one television masterpiece, in the sense of a work made for television without any collateral debt to the theatre, to the cinema, or to a published work of fiction, the indisputable claimant must be 'Upstairs, Downstairs,'" Alistair Cooke wrote in 1981.

"What gave it extraordinary distinction was the sure observation of character, the confidence and finesse with which social nuances and emotional upheavals between the two groups were explored, and the scrupulous accuracy of the period language, decor, mores, and prejudices."

At the time the series begins, the Bellamy family of four has eight servants: a butler, parlormaid, cook, ladies' maid, kitchen maid, chauffeur, and two footmen. The ratio of served to servers was, in fact, modest for this patrician age, when unemployment was high, and servants could count on security, a bed, and good food along with their wages of about £20 a year. For that, a servant worked 18 hours a day, six days a week, at the constant beck and call of the master's bell.

Much changed with World War I when the men went to battle and the women worked in factories. And, following the Crash in 1929, grand homes were auctioned off and servants became an intolerable luxury.

Jean Marsh (right) as Rose and Anne Yarker as Alice Hamilton.

Upstairs (right):
Richard Bellamy (David Langton).

Downstairs (below): Hudson (Gordon Jackson) reads the news at breakfast with (from left) Daisy (Jacqueline Tong), Rose, and Mrs. Bridges (Angela Baddeley).

UPSTAIRS, DOWNSTAIRS, Series II
(*13 episodes*)

November 3, 1974 – January 26, 1975
Repeat: May 11 – August 3, 1975

Produced by: London Weekend Television
Producer: John Hawkesworth
Script Editor: Alfred Shaughnessy

"Miss Forest"
Original drama by: Alfred Shaughnessy
Director: Bill Bain

"A House Divided"
Original drama by: Rosemary Anne Sisson
Director: Christopher Hodson

"A Change of Scene"
Original drama by: Rosemary Anne Sisson
Director: Bill Bain

"A Family Secret"
Original drama by: Alfred Shaughnessy
Director: Derek Bennett

"Rose's Pigeon"
Original drama by: Jeremy Paul
Director: Bill Bain

"Desirous of Change"
Original drama by: Fay Weldon
Director: Lionel Harris

"Word of Honour"
Original drama by: Anthony Skene
Director: Christopher Hodson

"The Bolter"
Original drama by: John Hawkesworth
Director: Cyril Coke

"Goodwill to All Men"
Original drama by: Deborah Mortimer
Director: Christopher Hodson

"What the Footman Saw"
Original drama by: Jeremy Paul
Director: Cyril Coke

"A Perfect Stranger"
Original drama by: Jeremy Paul
Director: Christopher Hodson

"Distant Thunder"
Original drama by: Alfred Shaughnessy
Director: Bill Bain

"The Sudden Storm"
Original drama by: John Hawkesworth
Director: Bill Bain

1974/75
Emmy Awards: Outstanding Drama Series:
UPSTAIRS, DOWNSTAIRS
Outstanding Actress in a Drama Series:
Jean Marsh, UPSTAIRS, DOWNSTAIRS
Outstanding Director – Drama Series:
Bill Bain, UPSTAIRS, DOWNSTAIRS
Special Classification –
Host: Alistair Cooke,
UPSTAIRS, DOWNSTAIRS

MURDER MUST ADVERTISE
(*4 episodes*)

October 6 – October 27, 1974
Repeat: August 10 – August 31, 1975

Produced by: BBC
Based on the novel by Dorothy L. Sayers
Dramatized by: Bill Craig
Producer: Richard Beynon
Director: Rodney Bennett

Starring: Ian Carmichael, Peter Bowles
& Gwen Taylor

COUNTRY MATTERS, Series I
(*4 episodes*)

February 2 – February 23, 1975

Produced by: Granada Television
Producer: Derek Granger

"The Higgler"
Based on the story by A. E. Coppard
Dramatized by: Hugh Leonard
Director: Richard Martin
Starring: Keith Drinkel

"The Black Dog"
Based on the story by A. E. Coppard
Dramatized by: James Saunders
Director: John Mackenzie
Starring: Jane Lapotaire

"The Watercress Girl"
Based on the story by A. E. Coppard
Dramatized by: Hugh Leonard
Director: Barry Davis
Starring: Susan Fleetwood

"The Mill"
Based on the story by H. E. Bates
Dramatized by: James Saunders
Director: Donald McWhinnie
Starring: Rosalind Ayres & Brenda Bruce

VIENNA 1900
(*6 episodes*)

March 2 – April 6, 1975

Produced by: BBC
Based on the stories by Arthur Schnitzler
Dramatized by: Robert Muller
Producer: Richard Beynon
Director: Herbert Wise
Music: Johann Strauss

Starring: Lynn Redgrave, Robert Stephens,
Dorothy Tutin & Fiona Walker

THE NINE TAILORS
(*4 episodes*)

April 13 – May 4, 1975

Produced by: BBC
Based on the novel by Dorothy L. Sayers
Dramatized by: Anthony Steven
Producer: Richard Beynon
Director: Raymond Menmuir
Music: Herbert Chappell

Starring: Ian Carmichael, Glyn Houston
& Donald Eccles

Upstairs, Downstairs

Channel 13 Sundays at 8:30pm

Mobil

Masterpiece Theatre

1974 Emmy winner 'best dramatic series'

Season of 1974-75

Rose, Hudson, and Ruby (Jenny Tomasin) at the seashore.

Upstairs, Downstairs (Part II)

"Upstairs, Downstairs" is about two mutually dependent worlds and the gap between them. Above stairs are Lady Marjorie and her husband Richard, a member of Parliament, and their two children, James and Elizabeth. Below stairs are the servants, headed by Hudson, the butler.

These worlds intersect on a daily – even minute-by-minute – basis in the relationship of servers and served. Then there are the undercurrents, as important in their own way as any formal relationship. Any crisis in the Bellamy family becomes central to the staff downstairs, sometimes as gossip, sometimes as a threat to their ordered lives. So quarrels reverberate. The Bellamys' daughter Elizabeth marries Lawrence Kirbridge, a poet, then has the marriage annulled, and the staff feels the tension upstairs. The tension becomes palpable when young James Bellamy has an affair with the Under House parlormaid, Sarah, and the family sends them off – him to India with the Army, her to the country with child.

But when King Edward comes to dinner, the household unites for a memorable evening. All of them will remember the red carpet, the eight courses capped by Baron d'Agneau de lait Persille, the game of bridge, and above all, the luster of royalty.

Because of Richard Bellamy's political career, the series gains in historical resonance: Characters in "Upstairs, Downstairs" talk about, and are affected by, what Alistair Cooke calls "a continuous wash and buffeting of events great and small, national crises, fads and festivals, the death of kings, stock market shenanigans, political scandals, the uproar of the suffragettes, the disruption of family life by the First World War, the General Strike, the coming to power of Labor governments, and eventually the Wall Street crash, the bell that tolled the end of the Bellamys' life."

But much of this, by the 1974-1975 season, is still to come. This unprecedented success has three more years to run on public television. By the 1977 season, when the Bellamys leave 165 Eaton Place, bankrupted by the Great Crash, the series' audience will swell to over one billion people worldwide.

In 1974-1975, "Upstairs, Downstairs" won its second straight Emmy for outstanding drama series; also winning Emmys were Jean Marsh as outstanding actress in a drama series, Bill Bain as outstanding director of a drama series, and Alistair Cooke in the special classification of host.

Right: Virginia (Hannah Gordon), second wife of Richard Bellamy (David Langton).

Below: Hazel (Meg Wynn Owen) with James Bellamy (Simon Williams).

SHOULDER TO SHOULDER
(6 episodes)

October 5 – November 9, 1975
Repeat: July 25 – August 29, 1976

Produced by: BBC and
Warner Brothers Television

Starring: Georgia Brown, Sian Phillips,
Patricia Quinn, Angela Down
& Michael Gough

"The Pankhurst Family"
Original drama by: Ken Taylor
Producer: Verity Lambert
Director: Waris Hussein

"Annie Kenney"
Original drama by: Alan Plater
Producer: Verity Lambert
Director: Waris Hussein

"Lady Constance Lytton"
Original drama by: Douglas Livingstone
Producer: Verity Lambert
Director: Waris Hussein

"Christabel Pankhurst"
Original drama by: Ken Taylor
Producer: Verity Lambert
Director: Moira Armstrong

"Outrage"
Original drama by: Hugh Whitemore
Producer: Verity Lambert
Director: Moira Armstrong

"Sylvia"
Original drama by: Ken Taylor
Producer: Verity Lambert
Director: Waris Hussein

NOTORIOUS WOMAN
(7 episodes)

November 16 – December 28, 1975
Repeat: June 6 – July 18, 1976

Produced by: BBC with
Warner Brothers Television
Original drama by: Harry W. Junkin
Producer: Pieter Rogers
Director: Waris Hussein
Music: Chopin's Piano Concerto No. 2

Starring: Rosemary Harris, George Chakiris,
Sinead Cusack & Jeremy Irons

Titles: "Misalliance", "Success", "Conflict",
"Trial", "Prelude", "Sonata" & "Resolution"

1975/76
Emmy Award:
Outstanding Lead Actress in a Limited Series:
Rosemary Harris, NOTORIOUS WOMAN

UPSTAIRS, DOWNSTAIRS, Series III
(13 episodes)

January 4 – March 28, 1976
Repeat: July 8 – September 30, 1976

Produced by: London Weekend Television
Producer: John Hawkesworth

"A Patriotic Offering"
Original drama by: Rosemary Anne Sisson
Director: Derek Bennett

"News from the Front"
Original drama by: John Hawkesworth
Director: Derek Bennett

"The Beastly Hun"
Original drama by: Jeremy Paul
Director: Bill Bain

"Women Shall Not Weep"
Original drama by: Alfred Shaughnessy
Director: Christopher Hodson

"Tug of War"
Original drama by: Rosemary Anne Sisson
Director: Derek Bennett

"Home Fires"
Original drama by: Jeremy Paul
Director: Bill Bain

"If You Were the Only Girl in the World"
Original drama by: John Hawkesworth
Director: Raymond Menmuir

"The Glorious Dead"
Original drama by: Elizabeth Jane Howard
Director: Raymond Menmuir

"Another Year"
Original drama by: Alfred Shaughnessy
Director: Cyril Coke

"The Hero's Farewell"
Original drama by: Rosemary Anne Sisson
Director: Bill Bain

"Missing, Believed Dead"
Original drama by: Jeremy Paul
Director: Christopher Hodson

"Facing Fearful Odds"
Original drama by: John Hawkesworth
Director: Raymond Menmuir

"Peace out of Pain"
Original drama by: Alfred Shaughnessy
Director: Christopher Hodson

1975/76
Emmy Awards: Outstanding Limited Series:
UPSTAIRS, DOWNSTAIRS
Outstanding Supporting Actor:
Gordon Jackson, UPSTAIRS, DOWNSTAIRS

CAKES AND ALE
(3 episodes)

April 4 – April 18, 1976

Produced by: BBC
Based on the novel by Somerset Maugham
Dramatized by: Harry Green
Producer: Richard Beynon
Director: Bill Hays

Starring: Michael Hordern, Judy Cornwell,
Mike Pratt & Peter Jeffrey

SUNSET SONG
(6 episodes)

April 25 – May 30, 1976
Repeat: August 23 – September 27, 1981

Produced by: BBC
Based on the novel by
Lewis Grassic Gibbons
Dramatized by: Bill Craig
Producer: Pharic Maclaren
Director: Moira Armstrong
Music: Thomas Wilson

Starring: Andrew Keir, Edith Macarthur,
Vivien Heilbron & James Grant

SHOULDER TO SHOULDER

1903: When women fought for the right to vote
Masterpiece Theatre
Sundays 9:00pm on PBS beginning October

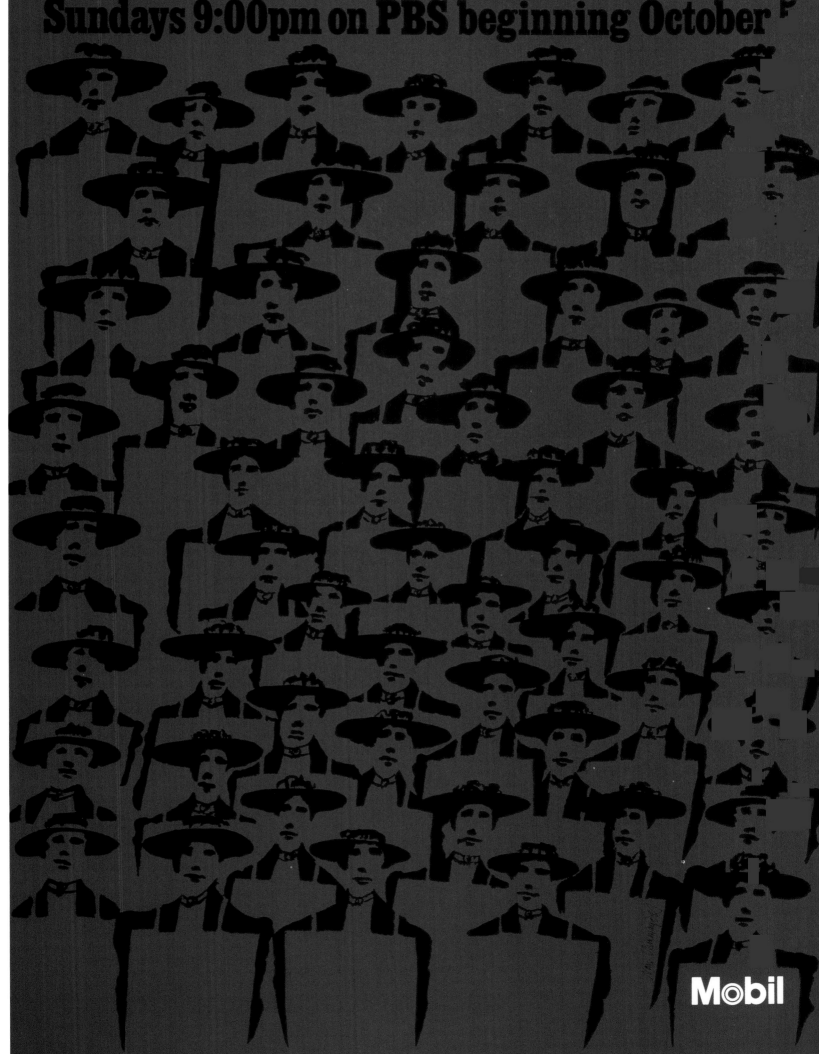

Mobil

Shoulder to Shoulder

"Next to property," said Emmeline Pankhurst, "the thing most sacred to Englishmen is sport."

Which is why the suffragettes poured acid on golf-course greens.

What made their protest so daring was that they didn't live in an age of guerrilla theatre. Emmeline Pankhurst was a Victorian lady who even wore proper hats and gloves to demonstrations.

But when the women were clubbed, jailed, and forced-fed, they realized civility didn't work. Stronger measures were called for – and these militant women were soon disrupting Parliament, battling police in the streets, blowing up buildings, and defacing works of art.

Their goal, to gain the vote for British women, was finally achieved in 1918 after Britain became immersed in a larger war. For the suffragettes, it was the culmination of a long fight, first sounded in 1792 when Mary Wollstonecraft published *A Vindication of the Rights of Women.*

"Shoulder to Shoulder" is a six-part drama based on the lives of Emmeline Pankhurst, her daughters Christabel and Sylvia, and other modern British suffragettes. The series was created by three British women – Verity Lambert, Midge Mackenzie, and Tony Award-winner Georgia Brown. Ms. Brown also stars as Annie Kenney, a millhand from Lancashire who was one of the few working-class women to become integral to the movement.

"They were fascinating, complex characters," says Brown. "In doing the series, we immersed ourselves in their lives. We even wore their laced-up corsets. You could say they raised our consciousness."

Michael Gough as Dr. Pankhurst.

Right: Patricia Quinn as Christabel Pankhurst.

Below, from left: Emmeline Pankhurst (Sian Phillips), Annie Kenney (Georgia Brown), and Christabel Pankhurst at a rally for women's suffrage.

MADAME BOVARY
(4 episodes)

October 10 – October 31, 1976

Produced by: BBC
Based on the novel by Gustave Flaubert
Dramatized by: Giles Cooper
Producer: Richard Beynon
Director: Rodney Bennett
Music: Dudley Simpson

Starring: Francesca Annis, Denis Lill,
Tom Conti & Ray Smith

HOW GREEN WAS MY VALLEY
(6 episodes)

November 7 – December 12, 1976
Repeat: December 21, 1977 – January 26, 1978

Produced by: BBC and
20th Century Fox Television
Based on the novel by Richard Llewellyn
Adapted by: Elaine Morgan
Producer: Martin Lisemore
Director: Ronald Wilson

Starring: Sian Phillips, Stanley Baker
& Rhys Powys

FIVE RED HERRINGS
(4 episodes)

December 19, 1976 – January 9, 1977
Repeat: August 20, 1977

Produced by: BBC
Based on the novel by Dorothy L. Sayers
Dramatized by: Anthony Steven
Producer: Bill Sellers
Director: Robert Tronson
Music: Herbert Chappell

Starring: Ian Carmichael & Glyn Houston

UPSTAIRS, DOWNSTAIRS, Series IV
(16 episodes)

January 16 – May 1, 1977
Repeat: September 5 – September 29, 1977

Produced by: London Weekend Television
Producer: John Hawkesworth
Script Editor: Alfred Shaughnessy

"On With the Dance"
Original drama by: Alfred Shaughnessy
Director: Bill Bain

"A Place in the World"
Original drama by: Jeremy Paul
Director: Christopher Hodson

"Laugh a Little Louder Please"
Original drama by: Rosemary Anne Sisson
Director: Derek Bennett

"The Joy Ride"
Original drama by: Alfred Shaughnessy
Director: Bill Bain

"Wanted, A Good Home"
Original drama by: John Hawkesworth
Director: Christopher Hodson

"An Old Flame"
Original drama by: John Hawkesworth
Director: Derek Bennett

"Disillusion"
Original drama by: Alfred Shaughnessy
Director: Bill Bain

"Such a Lovely Man"
Original drama by: Rosemary Anne Sisson
Director: Christopher Hodson

"The Nine Day Wonder"
Original drama by: Jeremy Paul
Director: Simon Langton

"The Understudy"
Original drama by: Jeremy Paul
Director: James Ormerod

"Alberto"
Original drama by: Alfred Shaughnessy
Director: Christopher Hodson

"Till Ye No Come Back Again"
Original drama by: Rosemary Anne Sisson
Director: Bill Bain

"Joke Over"
Original drama by: Rosemary Anne Sisson
Director: Bill Bain

"Noblesse Oblige"
Original drama by: John Hawkesworth
Director: Cyril Coke

"All the King's Horses"
Original drama by: Jeremy Paul
Director: Simon Langton

"Whither Shall I Wander"
Original drama by: John Hawkesworth
Director: Bill Bain

1976/77
Emmy Awards: Outstanding Drama Series:
UPSTAIRS, DOWNSTAIRS
Outstanding Continuing Performance by a
Supporting Actress in a Drama Series:
Jacqueline Tong,
UPSTAIRS, DOWNSTAIRS

POLDARK, Series I
(16 episodes)

May 8 – August 21, 1977
Repeat: July 2 – October 8, 1979 with
POLDARK, Series II

Produced by: BBC
Based on the novel by Winston Graham
Dramatized by: Jack Pulman, Paul Wheeler,
Peter Draper & Jack Russell
Producer: Morris Barry
Directors: Christopher Barry, Paul Annett
& Kenneth Ives

Starring: Robin Ellis, Jill Townsend,
Angharad Rees & Ralph Bates

Poldark

He returned from a lost war to fight for a new life.
Masterpiece Theatre
Sunday evenings on PBS
Beginning May 8

Mobil

Madame Bovary

"If the effects of a symphony have ever been conveyed in a book, it will be in these pages," Gustave Flaubert wrote to Louise Colet on August 26, 1853. "I want the reader to hear everything together, like one great roar – the bellowing of bulls, the sighing of lovers, the bombast of official oratory."

The scene – in which Flaubert juxtaposes the bombast of an agricultural fair to Emma Bovary's seduction by the manipulative Rodolphe – is one of the most memorable in literature. And Flaubert's novel, *Madame Bovary*, has been universally admired for its style, language and pitilessly objective treatment of the French bourgeoisie. In Emma Bovary, Flaubert creates a heroine lured – and destroyed – by the Romantic ideal he despises. When her dreams conflict with the humdrum reality of marriage to a dull, provincial doctor, she becomes enmeshed in affairs and financial excess.

Madame Bovary was, in its time, a shocking book. When it was published in 1856, the French government prosecuted Flaubert for obscenity. He was acquited because the court saw a cautionary moral in Emma's tragic end.

Flaubert meanwhile saw Emma's universality. "My poor Emma is living and suffering in towns and villages all over France at this moment," he wrote to a friend.

He had, in fact, derived Emma's story from a real-life case reported in the local press. The critic Sainte Beuve wrote that the novel had "the most hackneyed possible setting – the French provinces; the dullest people – the ordinary people of a country town; the most overworked theme in literature – adultery." From these familiar ingredients, Flaubert created his classic work.

Madame Bovary first appeared in serialized form – much like the episodes of Masterpiece Theatre. While *Madame Bovary* has often been produced on stage and in films, this is its first adaptation for television.

The London Sunday *Telegraph* wrote that it was "splendidly produced," and the *Daily Mail* judged it "as near a faultless classic serial as we're likely to encounter."

The *Telegraph* added that "Francesca Annis in the title role looks as though she was born for the part. Moving from one form of prison to another she is like some beautifully plumed bird flapping and breaking its wings on the rough rocks of life's reality."

Francesca Annis as Emma Bovary.

Emma and Charles Bovary, played by
Tom Conti, right and below, at their wedding.

DICKENS OF LONDON
(10 episodes)

August 28 – October 30, 1977

Produced by: Yorkshire Television
Original television series written by
Wolf Mankowitz
Producer: Marc Miller
Directors: Marc Miller &
Michael Ferguson

Starring: Roy Dotrice

I, CLAUDIUS
(13 episodes)

November 6, 1977 – January 29, 1978
Repeat: June 10 – September 2, 1979
Repeat: June 9 – August 25, 1991

Produced by: BBC, in association with
London Film Productions, Ltd.
Based upon the novels by Robert Graves
Dramatized by: Jack Pulman
Producer: Martin Lisemore
Director: Herbert Wise
Music: Wilfred Josephs

Starring: Derek Jacobi, Sian Phillips,
George Baker, John Hurt & Patrick Stewart

1977/78
Emmy Award:
Outstanding Art Director for a Drama Series:
Tim Harvey, Art Director, I, CLAUDIUS

ANNA KARENINA
(10 episodes)

February 5 – April 9, 1978
Repeat: August 1978

Produced by: BBC
Based on the novel by Leo Tolstoy
Dramatized by: Donald Wilson
Producer: Donald Wilson
Executive Producer: Ken Riddington
Director: Basil Coleman
Music: Glazounov's "Finnish Fantasy,"
Opus. 88

Starring: Nicola Pagett, Eric Porter,
Stuart Wilson & Robert Swann

OUR MUTUAL FRIEND
(7 episodes)

April 16 – May 28, 1978
Repeat: August 12 – September 23, 1979

Produced by: BBC
Based upon the novel by Charles Dickens
Adapted by: Julia Jones and
Donald Churchill
Producer: Martin Lisemore
Director: Peter Hammond

Starring: Leo McKern & John McEnery

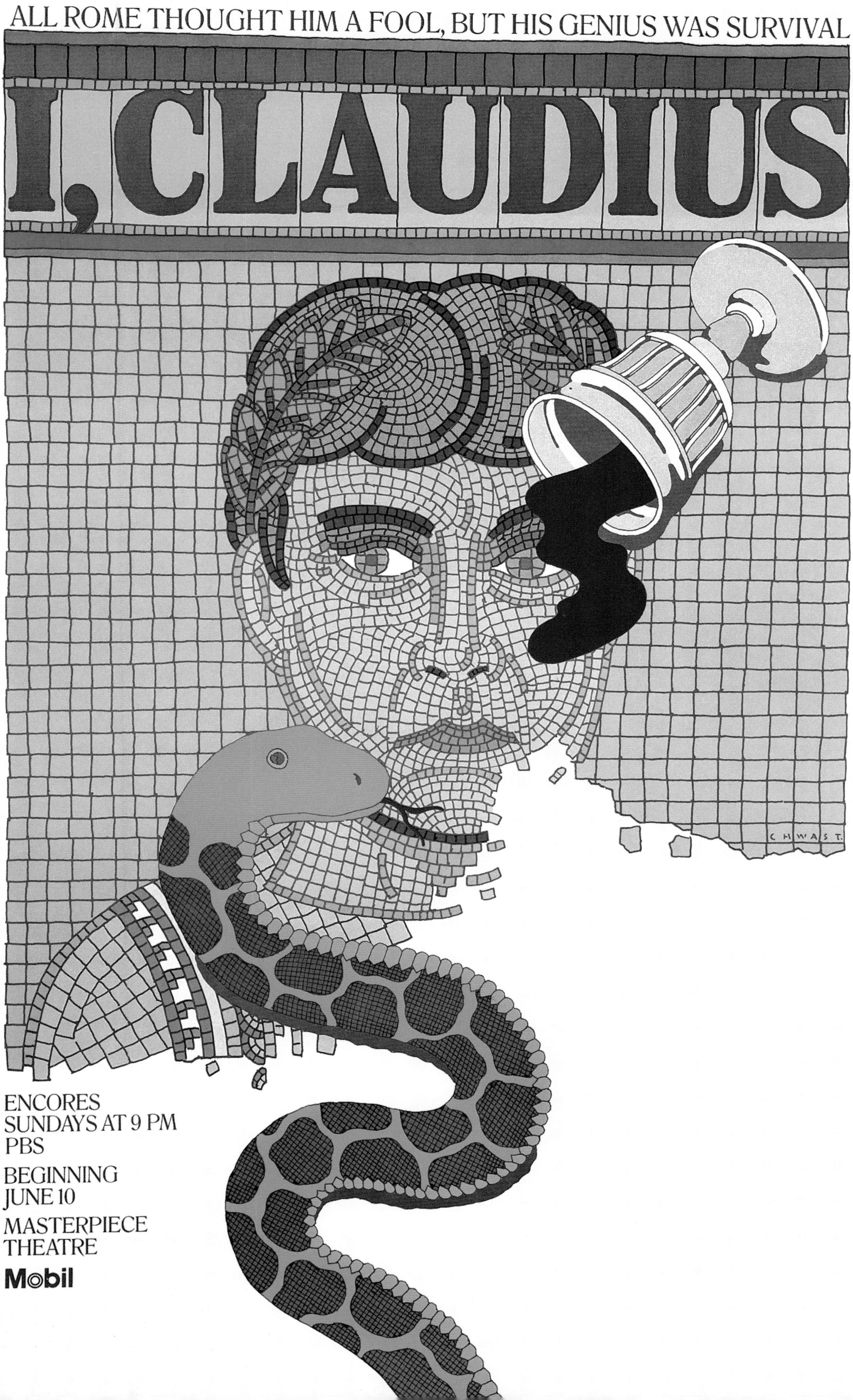
ALL ROME THOUGHT HIM A FOOL, BUT HIS GENIUS WAS SURVIVAL
I, CLAUDIUS
CHWAST.
ENCORES
SUNDAYS AT 9 PM
PBS
BEGINNING
JUNE 10
MASTERPIECE
THEATRE
Mobil

I, Claudius

"I, Tiberius Claudius Drusus Nero Germanicus This-that-and-the-other (for I shall not trouble you yet with all my titles) who was once, and not so long ago either, known to my friends and relatives and associates as 'Claudius the Idiot', or 'That Claudius', or 'Claudius the Stammerer', or 'Clau-Clau-Clau-Claudius', or at best 'Poor Uncle Claudius', am now about to write this strange history of my life."

So begins Robert Graves's audacious novel, *I, Claudius*. The story of the first four emperors of Rome, it is told in his old age by Claudius, a chronic stutterer and spastic who has survived, almost miraculously, to succeed Caligula on the throne.

Graves even claims that Claudius has written the book and left it with the prophetess Sibyl "for nineteen hundred years or so." Only then will it be revealed to readers who were previously unaware of some of the first emperors' perfidies or of Claudius' strengths.

His mock ingenuousness notwithstanding, Graves was an accomplished scholar who derived much of the material for *I, Claudius* and its successor, *Claudius, the God*, from Tacitus and Suetonius.

"Claudius' imperial record was unsurpassed by any other of the 12 Caesars except Augustus," Graves writes. He credits Claudius with "clearing up the mess left by his insane predecessor, Caligula ... strengthening the army, centralizing the Civil Service ... improving judicial procedure; bestowing on Rome an adequate water supply and a capacious harbor ..."

Claudius' predecessors do not fare as well. Even Augustus is upstaged by his wife Livia, who plots to have her son Tiberius succeed him. Tiberius is a lecher, Caligula a maniac, and intrigue, cruelty, corruption, and lust are the daily currency of Graves's ancient Rome.

When the work was adapted for television, there was trepidation about its reception by the normally squeamish American public. But this exceptional production earned only kudos.

The series, wrote Gerald Clarke in *Time*, "is little short of wonderful. Sian Phillips stands out as Livia, the wicked witch of the Tiber. Derek Jacobi's Claudius is half stumble and half stutter and half genius, but convincing in every detail."

Derek Jacobi as the future Emperor Claudius.

Right: Emperor Augustus (Brian Blessed) and his scheming wife Livia (Sian Phillips).

Below: Caligula (John Hurt) at the death bed of his great grandmother Livia.

Anna Karenina

At the autopsy of a young Russian woman who had thrown herself under a freight train, there was one witness: "a solid, stocky individual, with bushy eyebrows, heavy beard and flat nose, whose eyes shone with the flash of a mirror." The witness was Count Leo Tolstoy; as his biographer Henri Troyat relates: "He seemed to read a terrible lesson in her large, contracted eyes. He tried to imagine her life: a life given to sensual pleasures, ending in such a common, ugly manner."

Tolstoy was already undergoing what Troyat calls "a moral revolution," and the woman's death led him to write *Anna Karenina*. He saw in his heroine Anna a "folly of the senses." By pursuing her love for Count Vronsky, she sacrifices her marriage, her family, and her standing in society. For while society tolerates affairs, it expects discretion. Anna indiscreetly wants passion and acceptance.

And yet Tolstoy is never contemptuous of his heroine. The humanity that enriches all his work shines on Anna, even in her degradation.

While he takes the character of Anna from a chance corpse in a train station, Tolstoy draws on his own life when writing of the second pair of lovers, Anna's sister-in-law Kitty and the idealistic Levin. Levin, like Tolstoy, even proposes to his future wife by writing a cryptic message to her on a gambling table.

A master storyteller, Tolstoy built his audience's interest over two years of serialized installments. In adapting this long, dense novel to television, writer Donald Wilson telescopes events, keeping to "the spirit of the original" but reconstructing it as a visual drama.

Variety applauded "the glowing results," through which "Tolstoy's classic novel has been so sumptuously brought to life . . . As far as the cast of thousands go, all are excellent and have been masterfully selected. Nicola Pagett makes a stunning, silently sensuous heroine; Eric Porter, a near perfect mold of the insecure Karenin; Robert Swann, an instantly affecting Levin."

Nicola Pagett as Anna Karenina.

Right: Carole Nimmons as Dolly and Stuart Wilson as Anna's lover, Vronsky.

Below: Eric Porter plays her embittered husband, Karenin.

THE MAYOR OF CASTERBRIDGE
(7 episodes)

September 3 – October 15, 1978

Produced by: BBC
Based upon the novel by Thomas Hardy
Adapted by: Dennis Potter
Producer: Jonathan Powell
Director: David Giles
Music: Carl Davis

Starring: Alan Bates, Anna Massey,
Anne Stallybrass & Janet Maw

THE DUCHESS OF DUKE STREET,
Series I
(15 episodes)

October 22, 1978 – January 28, 1979

Produced by: BBC
Producer: John Hawkesworth
Music: Alexander Faris

Starring: Gemma Jones, Donald Burton,
& Christopher Cazanove

"A Bed of Roses"
Original drama by: John Hawkesworth
Director: Bill Bain

"For Love or Money"
Original drama by: John Hawkesworth
Director: Raymond Menmuir

"A Lady of Virtue"
Original drama by: Jeremy Paul
Director: Cyril Coke

THE DUCHESS OF DUKE STREET,
Series I con't.

"Trouble and Strife"
Original drama by: Jeremy Paul
Director: Raymond Menmuir

"The Outsiders"
Original drama by: Rosemary Anne Sisson
Director: Simon Langton

"Lottie's Boy"
Original drama by: Julia Jones
Director: Cyril Coke

"No Lawyers, No Letters"
Original drama by: Bill Craig
Director: Simon Langton

"A Matter of Honour"
Original drama by: Julian Bond
Director: Bill Bain

"One Night's Grace"
Original drama by: Ken Taylor
Director: Cyril Coke

"Plain Sailing"
Original drama by: Jeremy Paul
Director: Raymond Menmuir

"A Test of Love"
Original drama by: John Hawkesworth
Director: Bill Bain

COUNTRY MATTERS, Series II
(5 episodes)

February 4 – March 4, 1979

Produced by: Granada Television
Producer: Derek Granger

"Crippled Bloom"
Based on the story by: A. E. Coppard
Adapted by: Jeremy Paul
Director: Barry Davis
Starring: Pauline Collins & Joss Ackland

"Breeze Anstey"
Based on the story by: H. E. Bates
Adapted by: Hugh Whitemore
Director: Peter Wood
Starring: Morag Hood, Rachel Kempson &
Meg Wynn Owen

"The Simple Life"
Based on the story by: H. E. Bates
Adapted by: Hugh Whitemore
Director: Silvio Narizzano
Starring: Robert Urquhart, Peter Firth &
Maggie Fitzgibbon

"An Aspidistra in Babylon"
Based on the story by: H. E. Bates
Adapted by: Jeremy Paul
Director: Richard Everitt
Starring: Jeremy Brett & Carolyn Courage

"The Sullens Sisters"
Based on the story by: A. E. Coppard
Adapted by: Hugh Leonard
Director: Barry Davis
Starring: Clare Sutcliffe & Penelope Wilton

LILLIE
(13 episodes)

March 11 – June 3, 1979
Repeat: June 29 – September 21, 1980

Produced by: London Weekend Television
Starring: Francesca Annis, Denis Lill,
Peter Egan, Anton Rodgers & John Castle

"Emillie"
Original drama by: David Butler
Producer: Jack Williams
Director: John Gorrie

"Mrs. Langtry"
Original drama by: David Butler
Producer: Jack Williams
Director: John Gorrie

"The Jersey Lily"
Original drama by: David Butler
Producer: Jack Williams
Director: John Gorrie

"The New Helen"
Original drama by: David Butler
Producer: Jack Williams
Director: Christopher Hodson

"Bertie"
Original drama by: David Butler
Producer: Jack Williams
Director: Christopher Hodson

"Let Them Say"
Original drama by: David Butler
Producer: Jack Williams
Director: Christopher Hodson

"The Sailor Prince"
Original drama by: John Gorrie
Producer: Jack Williams
Director: John Gorrie

"Going on the Stage"
Original drama by: John Gorrie
Producer: Jack Williams
Director: Tony Wharmby

"America"
Original drama by: John Gorrie
Producer: Jack Williams
Director: John Gorrie

"Home on the Range"
Original drama by: David Butler
Producer: Jack Williams
Director: Tony Wharmby

"Mr. Jersey"
Original drama by: David Butler
Producer: Jack Williams
Director: John Gorrie

"Sunset and Evening Star"
Original drama by: David Butler
Producer: Jack Williams
Director: Tony Wharmby

"Fifty Cents a Dance"
Original drama by: John Gorrie
Producer: Jack Williams
Director: John Gorrie

Chermayeff & Geismar

Masterpiece Theatre *presents*

The Mayor of Casterbridge

starring Alan Bates

He was invincible—until his past began to haunt him

Sundays at 9pm beginning September 3 Channel 13 PBS

Mobil

The Mayor of Casterbridge

"Thomas Hardy is perhaps the greatest writer of rural life and landscape in the language," writes Margaret Drabble. "Other writers, observing from a distance, tend to see small farmers, labourers and day labourers lumped together in one undifferentiated mass, but Hardy's plots turn on the small distinctions, the rises and falls of country fortunes."

In recreating Hardy's *The Mayor of Casterbridge* for television, the BBC set back the clock by 140 years to transform a Dorset village into Hardy's fictional Casterbridge. Dorchester, the real model for Hardy's village, proved too busy for filmic alchemy. In neighboring Corfe Castle, however, the job was manageable, and horsedrawn wagons were soon tramping through cobblestoned streets.

Capturing the look of a great work of fiction is just one piece of the task of adapting it for television. The key, above all, was to get *inside* Hardy's mind and moral design.

The Mayor of Casterbridge is the story of a man who, like Oedipus, cannot escape his past. The man, Michael Henchard, has auctioned off his wife Susan and their daughter, only to be found out by them 18 years later. Formerly an unemployed farmer, he is now prosperous – and the Mayor of Casterbridge.

Though he tries to eradicate his sin by remarrying Susan, he cannot change his nature. He becomes jealous of his bookkeeper, a young Scot named Donald Farfrae who is in love with Susan's daughter, Elizabeth Jane. After firing Farfrae, he learns that the girl is not in fact his daughter. (That child died three months after he auctioned her off.)

After his wife dies, he seeks respectability by proposing to marry his former mistress, Lucetta. But coincidence destroys his name – and Lucetta's commitment to him – when an old woman appears before him in court and remembers the incident in which he sold off his family for a pittance.

Discredited, bankrupt, and alone, Henchard becomes a bitter recluse – affirming Hardy's Aristotelian view of tragedy.

Alan Bates as the Mayor of Casterbridge.

Bates as Michael Henchard, right and below, with Anna Massey as Lucetta.

Lillie

The daughter of an Anglican Dean from the Isle of Jersey, Lillie Langtry dreamed of gilded pleasures – and found them through her love affair with Bertie, Prince of Wales. She was the first acknowledged mistress of the Prince, who later became King Edward VII. And she used her notoriety, and Edward's support, to enter the great salons and attain a career as an actress and model.

She was the first woman to endorse a commercial product: Pears' Soap. "For the hands and complexion, I prefer Pears' to any other," she boasted in ads featuring her signature and her handsome profile.

Indeed, she was handsome. "To look at Lillie is to imagine one is dreaming," said James Whistler. "She is so extraordinary that not even I can do her justice in a painting."

But the woman dubbed the Jersey Lily had more than beauty: she had audacity, style, and intelligence. She could galvanize an entire ballroom by her entrance – though at first she owned only one formal dress. Oscar Wilde, her friend and admirer, convinced her that a London dressmaker would gladly make a dress free of charge for her. Wearing this second dress of white velvet, she caused another sensation.

Despite her social ambitions, she was no sycophant She rejected the advances of King Leopold of Belgium. And while still Prince Edward's mistress, she dropped ice down his collar when he rebuffed her at a ball.

In her youth, she had married Edward Langtry for his yachts and the chance to get away from Jersey. She soon found him profligate, moody, and a drunkard. Saddled with him, she turned first to Bertie, then to Bertie's nephew, Prince Louis of Battenberg.

Bertie ruled out any chance that Lillie would marry into royalty, but he remained her protector after she gave birth to Louis' daughter.

Until then, Lillie's triumphs had been social; now she turned to acting, first in London, then in America, where she became an overnight success. She also became wealthy.

And for a while, at least, she kept her beauty. Even George Bernard Shaw was impressed. "I resent Mrs. Langtry," he wrote. "She has no right to be intelligent, daring and independent as well as lovely. It is a frightening combination of attributes."

In her late forties, as her beauty faded, she married a tall, handsome, ineffectual baronet. She lived with him until she died in 1929.

Francesca Annis, who earlier played Madame Bovary on Masterpiece Theatre, is the stunning, insouciant Lillie.

Reviewing the series, Arthur Unger of the *Christian Science Monitor* wrote: "'Lillie' is bold and cheeky, and shows undertones of the changing male-female relationships during the period it portrays. It is entertaining television, perhaps a bit too boisterous for some tastes now and then, but, on the whole, a serious attempt to explain a woman and era too often forgotten as today's liberation movement forges ahead in its own way."

Lillie Langtry (Francesca Annis) pays homage to Queen Victoria (Sheila Reed).

Right: Peter Egan as Oscar Wilde, Lillie's friend and admirer.

Below: Lillie is attended by a new suitor, Squire Abington (Nicholas Jones).

KEAN
(2 episodes)

September 9 – 16, 1979

Produced by: BBC
Based on the play by Jean-Paul Sartre
Translated by: Frank Hauser
Producer: David Jones
Director: James Cellan Jones

Starring: Anthony Hopkins, Robert Stephens,
Cherie Lunghi & Neville Phillips

LOVE FOR LYDIA
(12 episodes)

September 23 – December 9, 1979

Produced by: London Weekend Television
Based on a novel by H. E. Bates
Dramatized by: Julian Bond
Producer: Tony Wharmby
Directors: Tony Wharmby (episodes 1, 2, 3, 6)
John Glenister (episode 4)
Piers Haggard (episode 7)
Michael Simpson (episode 8)
Simon Langton (episodes 9, 10)
Christopher Hodson (episodes 11, 12)
Music: Harry Rabinowitz

Starring: Mel Martin, Jeremy Irons,
Rachel Kempson & Peter Davison

THE DUCHESS OF DUKE STREET,
Series II
(16 episodes)

December 16, 1979 – April 6, 1980

Produced by: BBC-TV/Time-Life
Television co-production
Producer: John Hawkesworth

Starring: Gemma Jones
& Christopher Cazanove

"Family Matters"
Original drama by: Julia Jones
Director: Bill Bain

"Poor Catullus"
Original drama by: Jeremy Paul
Director: Cyril Coke

"A Lesson in Manners"
Original drama by: Rosemary Anne Sisson
Director: Cyril Coke

"Winter Lament"
Original drama by: Maggie Wadey
Director: Simon Langton

"The Passing Show"
Original drama by: John Hawkesworth
Director: Bill Bain

"Your Country Needs You"
Original drama by: John Hawkesworth
Director: Simon Langton

"The Patriots"
Original drama by: Bill Craig
Director: Bill Bain

"The Reluctant Warrior"
Original drama by: Rosemary Anne Sisson
Director: Simon Langton

"Tea and a Wad"
Original drama by: John Hawkesworth
Director: Cyril Coke

"Shadows"
Original drama by: Jeremy Paul
Director: Bill Bain

"Where There's a Will"
Original drama by: Julia Jones
Director: Cyril Coke

MY SON, MY SON
(7 episodes)

April 13 – May 25, 1980

Produced by: BBC
Based upon a novel by Howard Spring
Adapted by: Julian Bond
Producer: Keith Williams
Director: Peter Cregeen
Music: Rick Wakeman

Starring: Michael Williams, Patrick Ryecart,
Frank Grimes & Maurice Denham

DISRAELI: PORTRAIT OF A ROMANTIC
(4 episodes)

June 1 – June 22, 1980
Repeat: August 8 – August 29, 1982

Produced by: Independent TV
Corp/Associated TV
Based upon original material
Producer: Cecil Clarke
Director: Claude Whatham
Music: Wilfred Josephs

Starring: Ian McShane, Mary Peach
& Margaret Whiting

DISRAELI
PORTRAIT OF A ROMANTIC

Begins June 1
Sundays at 9 pm
Masterpiece Theatre
Channel 13, PBS

Mobil

Disraeli: Portrait of a Romantic

"I am a radical in order to uproot what is bad, a conservative to preserve what is good," is how Benjamin Disraeli described himself.

Others were less kind: He was denounced as an adventurer, a popinjay, a womanizer, a tawdry novelist, a social climber, a Jew who served in Parliament while English law still banned Jews from public office. (He qualified only because the family had converted to Christianity after his father quarreled with a Sephardic rabbi.)

His first speech before Parliament, in 1837, was a disaster. The words were pretentious, the man who delivered them looked like a dandy, and he was hooted down.

"I will sit down now but the time will come when you will hear me," he said.

Though his political career was not an instant success, he was proven right.

In part, he owed his success to women, who found him attractive, exotic, and eloquent. His first important supporter was the wife of Wyndham Lewis, a wealthy Conservative. Though he described her as "a frivolous rattle," he relished her influence, and became her second husband after Lewis' death.

He subsequently became a favorite of Queen Victoria, to whom he became "a dear and valued friend." By then, he had led a movement for Tory democracy, combining social justice and imperial might. He twice became Prime Minister. And he remained, long after his death, one of Britain's most controversial politicians.

In his review of the Masterpiece Theatre presentation, John O'Connor wrote in the *New York Times*: "'Disraeli' neatly juggles personal eccentricities and public events spanning several decades. Played by Ian McShane with a dark brooding intensity that might be deemed either smooth or oily, Dizzy is introduced as the elusive social lion with bill collectors quite literally at his door. While those around him fuss and flutter for his attention, he remains the calculating outsider, secure in the knowledge that in society you are not what you seem.

"Much of this 'Disraeli' is first rate. Mr. McShane brilliantly captures the character's ambition and genius. Mary Peach is adorable as the ostensibly flighty Mary Anne. And . . . the costumes and sets are splendid."

Ian McShane as Benjamin Disraeli.

Two of the women in Disraeli's life: Jenny Lipman as Sarah Disraeli (right), and Rosemary Leach as Queen Victoria.

Love for Lydia

In Britain, 1929 capped the Careless Twenties – a time of giddy prosperity. For Lydia Aspen, a provincial heiress, it is the time of her life. Dancing to the latest American tunes, flirting with four admirers, she is "always just ahead of her neighbors in acquiring the nervous sophistication of the 1920s, its fads and frivolities," says Alistair Cooke.

The heroine of H. E. Bates' *Love for Lydia* is careless in her affections, and even after two of her admirers die, she is unrepentant. Lydia, like a Chekhov heroine, is unaware that she is dancing on the edge of a precipice – for Britain's Threadbare Thirties will end the party for her and for the provincial Midlands town of Northamptonshire.

An acute observer of rural life, Bates was once dismissed by a publisher who found his early writings "Thomas Hardy with water."

Love for Lydia, a later work, is "a slow, bitter, relentless tale, Hardy with gall and wormwood," in the words of Alistair Cooke.

In this adaptation by London Weekend Television, the *Sunday Times* wrote: "The lives of two adjacent communities, nobs and yeomen living apart on almost feudal terms, were beautifully etched against a stark snow-covered Northamptonshire landscape."

The *Daily Telegraph* called the production "gorgeous to look at, the colours tinged with grey, blue and white and every scene flooded with a romantic air . . . And yet, there is a sense of reality, of actual presence, that is more than impressive. It is breathtaking."

*Jeremy Irons as Alex Sanderson and
Wendy Gifford as Mrs. Sanderson.*

Right: Rachel Kempson as Aunt Juliana.

Below: Jeremy Irons with Mel Martin as Lydia.

CRIME AND PUNISHMENT
(4 episodes)

September 28 – October 19, 1980

Produced by: BBC
Based upon the novel by
Fyodor Dostoyevsky
Adapted by: Jack Pulman
Producer: Jonathan Powell
Director: Michael Darlow

Starring: John Hurt, Sian Phillips,
Anthony Bate & Timothy West

PRIDE AND PREJUDICE
(5 episodes)

October 26 – November 23, 1980
Repeat: July 4 – August 1, 1982

Produced by: BBC
Based on the novel by Jane Austen
Dramatized by: Fay Weldon
Producer: Jonathan Powell
Director: Cyril Coke
Music: Wilfred Josephs

Starring: Elizabeth Garvie, David Rintoul,
Natalie Ogle & Clare Higgins

TESTAMENT OF YOUTH
(5 episodes)

November 30 – December 28, 1980
Repeat: September 5 – October 3, 1982

Produced by: BBC in association with London
Film Productions Ltd.
Based on the autobiography by Vera Brittain
Dramatized by: Elaine Morgan
Producer: Jonathan Powell
Director: Moira Armstrong

Starring: Cheryl Campbell, Rupert Frazer,
Joanna McCallum, Peter Woodward
& Rosalie Crutchley

DANGER UXB
(13 episodes)

January 4 – April 5, 1981

Produced by: Thames Television
Based on the book by Major Bill Hartley,
MBE, RE
Produced and created by: John Hawkesworth
Directors: Ferdinand Fairfax, Henry Herbert,
Simon Langton, Douglas Camfield,
Roy Ward Baker & Jeremy Summers

Starring: Anthony Andrews, Judy Geeson,
Maurice Roëves, Jeremy Sinden
& George Innes

THÉRÈSE RAQUIN
(3 episodes)

April 12 – 26, 1981
Repeat: July 7 – 21, 1983

Produced by: BBC and London Film
Productions Ltd. co-production
Based on the novel by Emile Zola
Dramatized by: Philip Mackie
Producer: Jonathan Powell
Director: Simon Langton
Music: Patrick Gowers

Starring: Kate Nelligan, Mona Washbourne,
Kenneth Cranham & Brian Cox

CRIME AND PUNISHMENT

Chernayeff & Geismar

Starring:
John Hurt *as Raskolnikov*
Timothy West *as the Examining Magistrate*

Sundays at 9 pm
Beginning September 28
PBS
Masterpiece Theatre

MASTERPIECE
THEATRE
10TH
ANNIVERSARY
SEASON 1980-81

Mobil

Crime and Punishment

"It is to be a psychological account of a crime. The action is contemporary, this year [1865]. A young man – Raskolnikov – of petit-bourgeois background has been expelled from the university and is living in extreme poverty. Lacking seriousness and stability in his mental make-up, he has given himself over to certain strange ideas in the air at that time. He determines to escape from his vile situation at one stroke: to murder an old woman who lends him money for interest, and with that money to bring happiness to his mother . . ."

In this brief letter to his publisher, Fyodor Dostoyevsky describes his Nietzschean detective story, *Crime and Punishment*. By killing an old pawnbroker, Raskolnikov hopes to prove that an extraordinary man is above the law. The events in the novel will prove him wrong.

Pursued by an examining magistrate, he succumbs to guilt. And eventually he finds redemption through punishment.

While the novel is set in St. Petersburg, the television series was shot at the Naval College in Greenwich, on the grounds of a house near Salisbury, and in an Edinburgh tenement.

Calling the production "a triumphant landmark in television drama," Martin Jackson writes in the *Daily Mail*: "It has stretched and extended the small screen in a most extraordinary way, miraculously transforming the Greenwich waterfront into a bustling replica of St. Petersburg in the 1860s."

He continues: "John Hurt's Raskolnikov is a magnificent portrayal, the remorseless inner struggle etched in that gaunt, tortured face."

After their successful collaboration in "I, Claudius," Hurt had suggested the adaptation to the late Jack Pulman. The outcome, writes Sean Day-Lewis in the *Daily Telegraph*, is "a triumphant memorial to its skilled adaptor, Jack Pulman."

John Hurt as Raskolnikov.

Right: Yolande Palfrey as Sonia, the saintly prostitute, and Timothy West as Porfiry, the examining magistrate.

Below: Raskolnikov with his mother (Yvonne Coulette).

Pride and Prejudice

Virginia Woolf called her "the most perfect artist among women, the writer whose books are immortal." Yet for much of her life, she hid her talent, writing discreetly in the family sitting room, and treating her work as an entertainment for family readings.

She was in her mid-thirties, with only a few years to live, when her first novel was published. It was her third novel that prompted one otherwise contemptuous neighbor to remark that "until *Pride and Prejudice* showed what a precious gem was hidden in that unbending case, she was no more regarded in society than a poker or firescreen . . . The case is very different now; she is still a poker – but a poker of whom everybody is afraid."

Jane Austen wrote the first draft of *Pride and Prejudice* when she was 21, then waited 15 years to rewrite it.

The book's main issue is framed in its first sentence: "It is a truth universally acknowledged, that a single man in possession of a good fortune must be in want of a wife."

The Bennets are keen to put this premise to the test, for they have five marriageable daughters. "They're all silly and ignorant," says their father, "but Lizzie [Elizabeth, the heroine] has something more of quickness than her sisters."

This quickness puts off potential suitors, and sets up a romantic faceoff, until late in the novel, between Elizabeth and the arrogant Mr. Darcy.

Fay Weldon, who adapted the novel, writes: "It has a many-layered density. You begin with what seems to be a small, beautifully neat book, exquisitely confined, and, as you work on it, it swells up like rice . . . [and] you respond to the other layers, to the skill of the writing, the fineness of the observation."

Reviewing the TV production of "Pride and Prejudice," John O'Connor writes in the *New York Times*: "the brittle romance of clever Elizabeth (Elizabeth Garvie) and proud Darcy (David Rintoul) remains a model of charm, distinctively British. As usual in a BBC production, the sets and costumes are splendid, and the performances are of an impressively high caliber."

Tessa Peake-Jones as Mary Bennet.

Right: The proud lovers, Elizabeth Bennet (Elizabeth Garvie) and Fitzwilliam Darcy (David Rintoul).

Below: Elizabeth's sisters Lydia (Natalia Ogle, left) and Kitty (Clare Higgins).

A TOWN LIKE ALICE
(6 episodes)

October 4 – November 8, 1981
Repeat: July 3 – August 7, 1983

Produced by: Alice Productions Pty Ltd. in association with The Seven Network Australia, The Australian Film Commission, The Victoria Film Corporation
Based on the novel by Nevil Shute
Dramatized by: Rosemary Anne Sisson and Tom Hegarty
Producer: Henry Crawford
Director: David Stevens
Music: Bruce Smeaton

Starring: Bryan Brown, Helen Morse & Gordon Jackson

EDWARD AND MRS. SIMPSON
(7 episodes)

November 15 – December 27, 1981

Produced by: Thames Television
Based on original material by Simon Raven
Producer: Andrew Brown
Associate Producer: Brenda Ennis
Director: Waris Hussein

Starring: Cynthia Harris, Edward Fox, Peggy Ashcroft & Patricia Hodge

THE FLAME TREES OF THIKA
(7 episodes)

January 3 – February 14, 1982
Repeat: August 14 – September 25, 1983

Produced by: Euston Films in association with Consolidated Productions for Thames Television
Based on the memoir by Elspeth Huxley
Adapted by: John Hawkesworth
Producers: John Hawkesworth & Christopher Neame
Director: Roy Ward Baker
Music: Ken Howard & Alan Blaikley

Starring: Hayley Mills, David Robb, Holly Aird & Ben Cross

I REMEMBER NELSON
(4 episodes)

February 21 – March 14, 1982

Produced by: ATV
Based on the screenplay by Hugh Whitemore
Producer: Cecil Clarke
Director: Simon Langton
Music: Patrick Gowers

Starring: Kenneth Colley, Geraldine James, Anna Massey & Tim Pigott-Smith

LOVE IN A COLD CLIMATE
(8 episodes)

March 28 – May 16, 1982

Produced by: Thames Television
Based upon the books by Nancy Mitford
Adapted by: Simon Raven
Producer: Gerald Savory
Director: Donald McWhinnie
Music: Julian Slade

Starring: Judi Dench, Michael Aldridge, Lucy Gutteridge, Vivian Pickles & Michael Williams

FLICKERS
(6 episodes)

May 23 – June 27, 1982
Repeat: July 28 – September 1, 1983

Produced by: ATV
Based upon original material by Roy Clarke
Producer: Joan Brown
Director: Cyril Coke
Music: Ron Grainer

Starring: Bob Hoskins & Frances de la Tour

Nevil Shute's
A TOWN LIKE ALICE

The war
changed them.
The outback
tested them.

Starring Bryan Brown and Helen Morse
Special guest star Gordon Jackson
Mobil Masterpiece Theatre begins October 4
Sunday evenings at 9pm Channel 13 PBS

Chermayeff & Geismar

Mobil

A Town Like Alice

In the U.S., "A Town Like Alice" was the first Australian-made series to appear on Masterpiece Theatre, and it came with the highest recommendations: In Australia, it had attracted 70% of all television viewers – a record for a home-grown series. And in the U.K., it had drawn 30% of the audience – close to the record for a mini-series. At that time, the London *Observer* wrote: "There has not been a richer story told on television for some time by anybody."

Based on a novel by Nevil Shute, "A Town Like Alice" is the love story of two prisoners of war incarcerated in Malaya by the Japanese. The heroine, an Englishwoman named Jean Paget, has survived six months of a forced march during which many women and children have died. She falls in love with Joe Harman, an Australian who is tortured – and ostensibly killed – after the Japanese catch him stealing chickens.

Seven years later, Jean returns to Malaya to build a well in a village where she eventually found refuge from the Japanese. While there, she learns that Joe is alive.

She heads off for Alice Springs, the town in the Australian Outback he has described fondly to her. He, meanwhile, has gone off to England to seek her.

They meet at last in Alice Springs, where their love revives after a false start.

The lovers are played by Australian film stars Bryan Brown and Helen Morse. The cast also features Gordon Jackson, best known as Hudson in "Upstairs, Downstairs."

Shute's idea for *A Town Like Alice* took shape during his visit to the Outback in 1948. In Sumatra, he subsequently met a woman whose experience during World War II mirrored Jean Paget's. There, the Japanese Army had subjected its captives to a death march because no women's camp existed.

A Town Like Alice is one of two Shute novels set in Australia. In the other, his apocalyptic *On the Beach*, the last survivors of atomic war gravitate there against the spread of radiation.

Helen Morse as Jean Paget and Bryan Brown as Joe Harman.

Right: Jean Paget and her captor, Mifune (Yuki Shimode), in war-torn Malaya.

Below: Paget adopts a child, Robyn Holland (Melissa Crawford).

The Flame Trees of Thika

Elspeth Huxley was 11 when she and her parents, Tilly and Robin Grant, arrived in Africa. Almost half a century later, in her memoir *The Flame Trees of Thika*, she recalls:

"We set off in an open cart drawn by four whip-scarred little oxen and piled high with equipment and provisions . . . We are going to Thika, a name on a map where two rivers joined."

This virgin territory in the East Africa Protectorate (now Kenya) was, indeed, little more than a name on a map. The Grants had been assured it was a coffee grower's paradise; they soon realized they had been conned.

"They had to dam streams for water and watch out for wart hogs and pythons and hyenas and let the Kikuyu (a local tribe) build their idea of a house, which leaked like a drain when the rains first came," Alistair Cooke recounts.

The Flame Trees of Thika became a best-seller when it was published in 1959. Another 20 years later, television producer and writer John Hawkesworth read the novel on a plane en route to Africa.

He soon returned to Africa to film the adaptation of "The Flame Trees of Thika." With him was the series' consultant, Elspeth Huxley.

She found "a country of wide-stretching plains speckled with thorn trees, beneath a rocky bluff frequented by baboons and, it was said, a solitary black leopard."

Much had changed, though the stone bungalow the Grants had built in 1914 was still there.

What had disappeared, above all, were the colonial underpinnings that had supported the Grants' time in Africa.

Huxley's Africa, in "The Flame Trees of Thika," centers on the Grants and their neighbors, the Palmers. In the story, recounted by 11-year-old Elspeth, the Grants learn to adapt: working with their hands, accepting the hard life, understanding tribal customs, keeping a wary eye out for leopards, rhinos, and lions. The Palmers do not adapt to the threats and the stimulation of their new environment. Lettice Palmer has an affair with a game hunter. And their lives are on the brink of crisis just when England and Germany declare war.

Africa, and the world, will never be the same.

"The Flame Trees of Thika" evokes a lost world; it "bursts on to our screens with all the warmth and brilliance of the African sun," wrote the London *Daily Express* reviewer.

The Grant family (from left): Robin (David Robb), Elspeth (Holly Aird), and Tillie (Hayley Mills).

Right: Sharon Mughan as Mrs. Palmer and Ben Cross as Ian Crawfurd.

Below: Elspeth with Mr. Ross (Morgan Sheppard).

TO SERVE THEM ALL MY DAYS
(13 episodes)

October 10, 1982 – January 2, 1983
Repeat: June 17 – September 9, 1984

Produced by: BBC, with Australian Film Commission
Based on the novel by R. F. Delderfield
Dramatized by: Andrew Davies
Producer: Ken Riddington
Director: Ronald Wilson

Starring: John Duttine, Belinda Lang & Frank Middlemas

THE GOOD SOLDIER
(Single 2-hour episode)

January 9, 1983
Repeat: June 3, 1984

Produced by: Granada Television
Based on the novel by Ford Madox Ford
Dramatized by: Julian Mitchell
Producer: Peter Eckersley
Director: Kevin Billington

Starring: Jeremy Brett, Susan Fleetwood, Robin Ellis & Vickery Turner

WINSTON CHURCHILL – THE WILDERNESS YEARS
(8 episodes)

January 16 – March 6, 1983
Repeat: August 24 – October 12, 1986

Produced by: Southern Pictures
Original drama by: Richard Broke & Martin Gilbert
Producer: Richard Broke
Director: Ferdinand Fairfax

Starring: Robert Hardy, Sian Phillips, Nigel Havers, Peter Barkworth & Eric Porter

ON APPROVAL
(Single 2-hour episode)

March 13, 1983
Repeat: March 11, 1984

Produced by: BBC
Original drama by: Frederick Lonsdale
Producer: Cedric Messina
Director: David Giles

Starring: Penelope Keith, Jeremy Brett, Lindsay Duncan & Benjamin Whitrow

DRAKE'S VENTURE
(Single 2-hour episode)

March 27, 1983
Repeat: June 10, 1984

Produced by: Westward Television
Original drama by: John Nelson Burton
Producer: Lawrance Gordon-Clark
Director: Lawrance Gordon-Clark

Starring: John Thaw, Paul Darrow & Charlotte Cornwell

PRIVATE SCHULTZ
(5 episodes)

April 3 – May 8, 1983
Repeat: September 1 – October 21, 1984

Produced by: BBC
Original drama by: Jack Pulman
Producer: Philip Hinchcliffe
Director: Robert Chetwyn

Starring: Ian Richardson, Michael Elphick, Billie Whitelaw & Rula Lenska

SONS AND LOVERS
(7 episodes)

May 15 – June 26, 1983

Produced by: BBC/co-production with 20th Century Fox
Based on the novel by D. H. Lawrence
Dramatized by: Trevor Griffiths
Producer: Jonathan Powell
Director: Stuart Burge
Music: John Tams

Starring: Eileen Atkins, Karl Johnson & Tom Bell

Winston Churchill: The Wilderness Years

He lost favor, brooded, fought and waited.
The time before his finest hour.

Starring Robert Hardy as *Winston*
Sian Phillips as *Clementine*

Mobil Masterpiece Theatre
Beginning January 16
Sundays at 9pm Channel 13 PBS

Mobil

Sons and Lovers

"*Sons and Lovers* is a work of autobiographical fiction that charts, with extraordinary fidelity, the events, circumstances and social relations of [D. H.] Lawrence's early life," writes Trevor Griffiths, who adapted the novel for the BBC. "Written between 1910 and 1912, it covers the period 1875-1910 through the lives of a mining family in Bestwood in Nottinghamshire, and especially through the emerging moral consciousness of Paul Morel, the novel's central figure, whose life differs in few important details from Lawrence's own."

In *Sons and Lovers*, Paul Morel is a spiritual outcast from this harsh coal-mining community and from his brutal, hard-drinking father. He is encouraged and cosseted by his mother, but the intensity of their relationship impedes his capacity to love another woman. Calling him "one of the more unabashed mama's boys of English literature," John O'Connor writes in the *New York Times*, "Paul will have tortured relations with the saintly Miriam, whom he doesn't even kiss for several years, and the more worldly Clara, a feminist who has left her bullying husband."

Only the death of his mother will finally liberate Paul — despite his pain at the book's end.

In adapting the novel for television, the BBC filmed in Lawrence's hometown of Nottinghamshire. The production captures the harsh environment that Lawrence left behind with the publication of *Sons and Lovers*.

Owen McNally of the *Hartford Courant* wrote that the production is "Masterpiece Theatre at its best, a tale of love, lust, friendship, betrayal, adultery, [and] fornication." In all, he said, it "has much to say about the human condition, love, loyalty, loneliness and death."

Ian Kirby as young Paul Morel and Eileen Atkins as his mother, Gertrude.

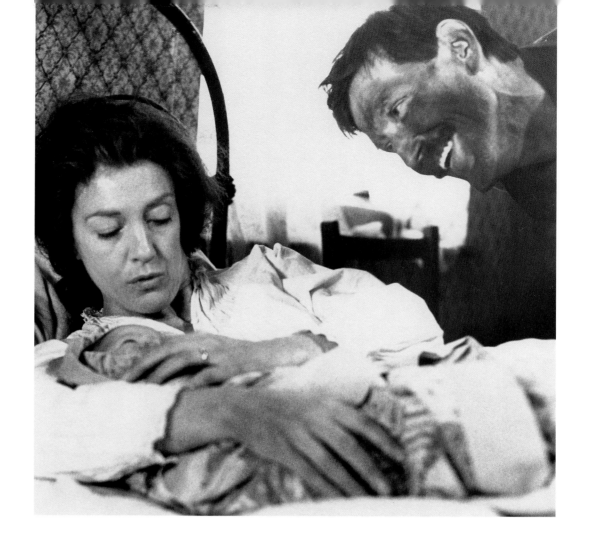

Right and below: Walter Morel (Tom Bell) at his wife's bedside, and giving away his daughter Annie (Amanda Parfitt).

PICTURES
(7 episodes)

October 2 – November 13, 1983

Produced by: Central Independent Television
Original drama by: Roy Clarke
Producer: Joan Brown
Director: Carol Wiseman

Starring: Wendy Morgan, Peter McEnery
& Anton Rodgers

THE CITADEL
(10 episodes)

November 20, 1983 – January 22, 1984
Repeat: June 23 – August 25, 1985

Produced by: BBC
Based on the novel by A. J. Cronin
Dramatized by: Don Shaw
Producer: Ken Riddington
Director: Mike Vardy

Starring: Ben Cross, Clare Higgins
& Gareth Thomas

THE IRISH R.M., Series I
(6 episodes)

January 29 – March 4, 1984
Repeat: September 1 – October 6, 1985

Produced by: Little Bird in association with
Ulster Television and
Radio Telefis Eireann
Based on works by: Somerville and Ross
Dramatized by: Rosemary Anne Sisson
Producers: Adrian Hughes & James Mitchell
Director: Robert Chetwyn

Starring: Peter Bowles, Faith Brook
& Lise-Ann McLaughlin

THE TALE OF BEATRIX POTTER
(2 episodes)

March 25 – April 1, 1984
Repeat: March 9, 1986
Repeat: September 27 – October 4, 1987

Produced by: BBC in association with
Consolidated Films
Original drama by: John Hawkesworth
Producer: Carol Robertson
Director: Bill Hays

Starring: Penelope Wilton & Holly Aird

NANCY ASTOR
(8 episodes)

April 8 – May 27, 1984

Produced by: A BBC Television/Time-Life
Films co-production
Original drama by: Derek Marlowe
Producer: Philip Hinchcliffe
Director: Richard Stroud

Starring: Lisa Harrow, Pierce Brosnan,
Nigel Havers & James Fox

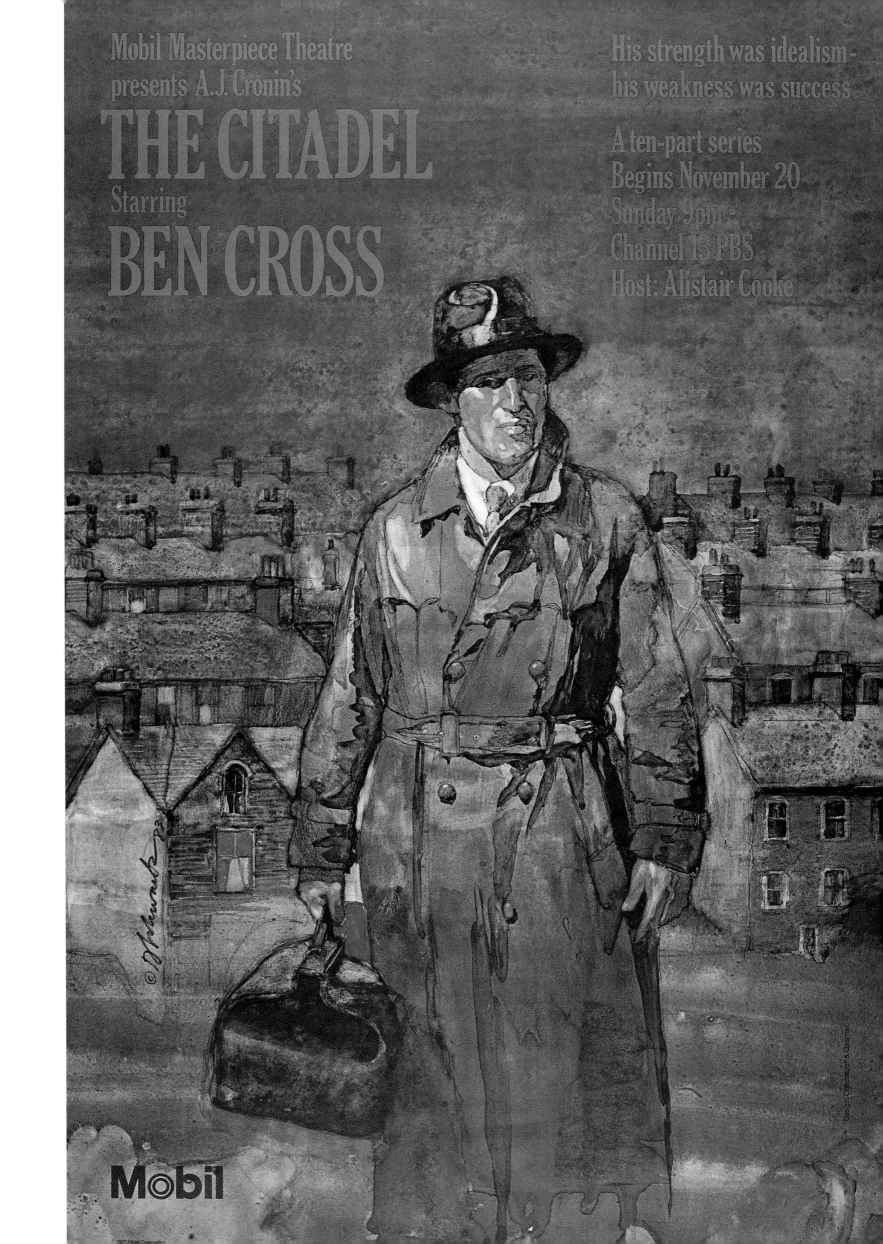

Mobil Masterpiece Theatre
presents A.J. Cronin's

THE CITADEL
Starring
BEN CROSS

His strength was idealism—
his weakness was success

A ten-part series
Begins November 20
Sunday 9pm
Channel 13 PBS
Host: Alistair Cooke

Mobil

The Citadel

"The horrors and inequities detailed in the story I have personally witnessed," author A. J. Cronin said in defense of his best-selling novel, *The Citadel*. "This is not an attack against individuals but against a system."

The "system" was the British medical establishment in the late 1930s. And the British Medical Association was outraged. They bought 200 copies of the book (out of 25 million it sold worldwide) and debated it at their 1937 conference. The debate was onesided: they agreed the book was "a piece of dramatized pamphleteering."

Dr. Cronin wasn't surprised. He had written the book from his own experience as a doctor in Wales and later in London. His main character, Dr. Andrew Manson, had, like Cronin himself, begun his practice in a Welsh mining town where local doctors turned a blind eye to the miners' chronic lung problems. Dr. Manson's crusade against silicosis, a miner's disease, continued long after he left the mining town. So too did his opposition to the greed and indifference of the British medical establishment.

In adapting *The Citadel* to television, the BBC production team shot the early scenes on location in the Rhonnda coal mining valley in Wales.

Later scenes occur in London, where Dr. Manson works, first for the Coal Mines Fatigue Board and later in a lucrative practice, where he sells out his own ideals and compromises his marriage.

In the final episode, however, Dr. Manson is "shocked into redemption by seeing the smartest surgeon he knows butcher an operation and kill the patient," says Alistair Cooke. "Manson recovers his senses, his idealism, and his splendid wife."

Harriet Van Horne, in *Newsday*, called the TV drama "the stern stuff of real life."

And John O'Connor of the *New York Times* applauded this "fine adaptation," and said that "Manson is played to grim but winning perfection by Ben Cross."

Ben Cross as the principled Dr. Andrew Manson.

Right: Preston Lockwood as Dr. Gadsby.

Below: Dr. Manson with his wife Christine (Clare Higgins).

THE BARCHESTER CHRONICLES
(7 episodes)

October 28 – December 9, 1984

Produced by: BBC
Based on Anthony Trollope's
The Warden and *Barchester Towers*
Dramatized by: Alan Plater
Producer: Jonathan Powell
Director: David Giles

Starring: Susan Hampshire,
Donald Pleasence, Geraldine McEwan,
Nigel Hawthorne & Janet Maw

THE JEWEL IN THE CROWN
(14 episodes; episode 1, 2 hours)

December 16, 1984 – March 17, 1985
Repeat: May 24 – August 23, 1987

Produced by: Granada Television
Based on Paul Scott's *The Raj Quartet*
Dramatized by: Ken Taylor
Producer: Christopher Morahan
Directors: Christopher Morahan &
Jim O'Brien
Music: George Fenton

Starring: Dame Peggy Ashcroft, Art Malik,
Judy Parfitt, Susan Wooldridge,
Geraldine James, Tim Pigott-Smith,
Charles Dance & Rachel Kempson

1984/85
Emmy Awards:
Outstanding Limited Series:
THE JEWEL IN THE CROWN
International Emmy: Best Drama:
THE JEWEL IN THE CROWN
– Special Classification:
The Governors' Award:
Alistair Cooke

ALL FOR LOVE
(5 episodes)

March 31 – April 28, 1985

Produced by: Granada Television

"A Dedicated Man"
Based on the novel by Elizabeth Taylor
Dramatized by: Hugh Whitemore
Producer: Roy Roberts
Director: Robert Knights

Starring: Joan Plowright & Alec McGowen

"Mona"
Based on the novel by Francis King
Dramatized by: Thomas Ellice
Producer: Roy Roberts
Director: Robert Knights

Starring: Frank Finlay & Deborah Stokes

"L'Elegance"
Based on the novel by Rumer Godden
Dramatized by: Lee Langley
Producer: Roy Roberts
Director: Jack Gold

Starring: Geraldine McEwan &
Jean Francois Stevenin

"A Bit of Singing and Dancing"
Based on the novel by Susan Hill
Dramatized by: Hugh Whitemore
Producer: Roy Roberts
Director: Robert Knights

Starring: June Ritchie & Evelyn Laye

"Letting the Birds Go Free"
Based on the novel by Philip Oakes
Dramatized by: Stephen Wakelam
Producer: Roy Roberts
Director: Moira Armstrong

Starring: Lionel Jeffries, Carolyn Pickles &
Tom Wilkinson

STRANGERS AND BROTHERS
(7 episodes)

May 5 – June 10, 1985

Produced by: BBC
Based on the novel by C. P. Snow
Dramatized by: Julian Bond
Producer: Philip Hinchcliffe
Directors: Ronald Wilson &
Jeremy Summers

Starring: Shaughan Seymour, Sheila Ruskin
& Nigel Havers

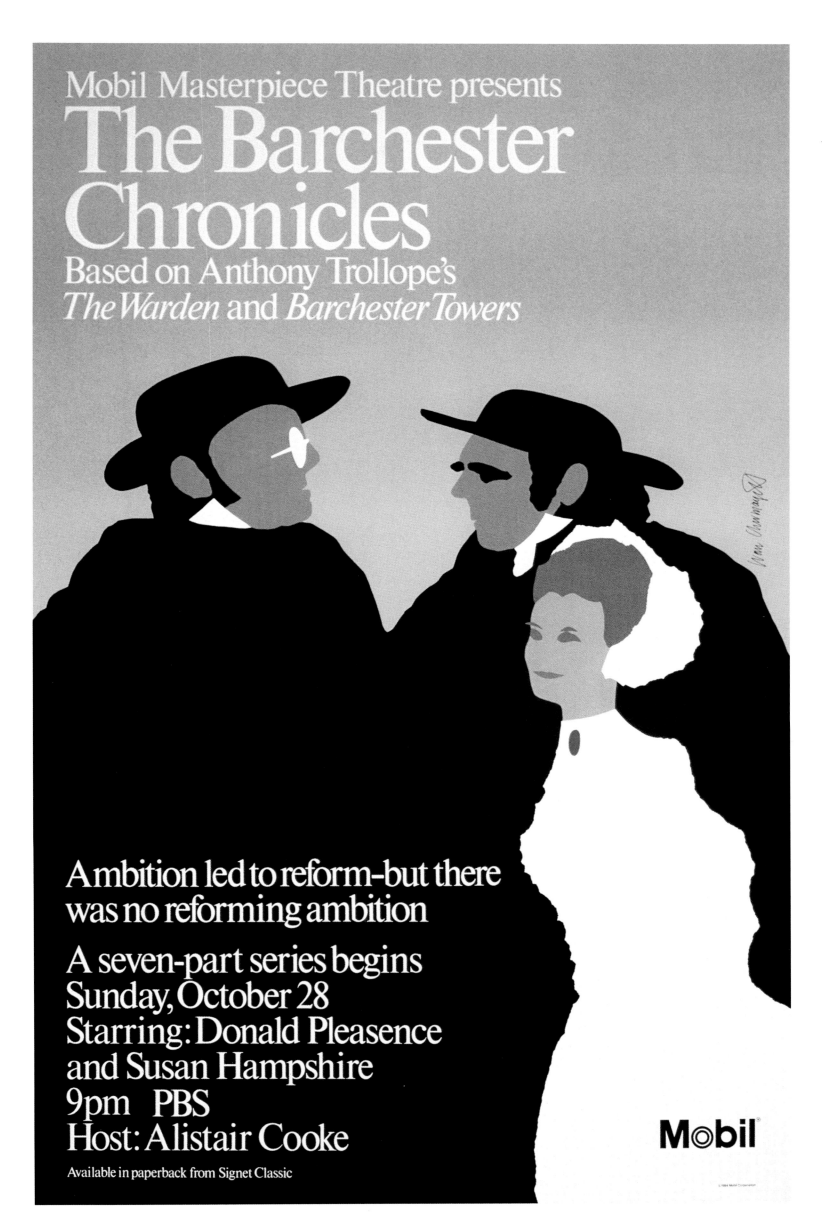

The Jewel in the Crown

"In 1942, which was the year the Japanese defeated the British army in Burma and Mr. Gandhi began preaching sedition in India," writes Paul Scott in *The Raj Quartet*, "the English then living in the civil and military cantonment of Mayapore had to admit that the future did not look propitious."

Of course they were right. For though the British won the war, they lost the Empire; and by 1948, most of them were gone from India.

In almost 2,000 pages of dense prose and changing perspectives, Scott's quartet spans six years in the death in the Raj. While reshaping his narrative into a linear form, the television adaptation, titled "The Jewel in the Crown," is as rich, exotic, and full of vivid characters as Scott's original.

"As enthralling episode follows enthralling episode, it sometimes seems to me that 'The Jewel in the Crown' is not just the series of the decade but the richest television drama of all," Sean Day-Lewis wrote in the *Daily Telegraph*.

American critics concurred. John O'Connor of the *New York Times* praised this "superb drama of reverberating substance," and John Leonard of *New York* magazine called the series "the best sustained television I've seen in more than 30 years of watching."

The rape of an English girl, Daphne Manners, is the first pivotal incident. A young Indian, Hari Kumar, is arrested and beaten while in jail by the local police superintendent, Ronald Merrick.

Later, Daphne dies in childbirth, Kumar languishes in prison, and Merrick becomes a soldier and the book's ubiquitous, evil presence – "holding together the entire series with the black magic of a self-made Iago," writes Pico Iyer in *Time* magazine.

The working-class Merrick is an outcast in the privileged world of colonial India. Throughout the series, his relations with British and Indians are almost unfailingly hostile. He finally ingratiates himself with the Laytons, a military family who dominate the second half of the series. But just after he marries Susan Layton, he is murdered in retribution for his treatment of Hari Kumar.

Tim Pigott-Smith as Merrick shares acting honors with a host of memorable performers. Iyer singles out three women: Susan Wooldridge as Daphne "galumphs through life with such sweet diffidence that plainness itself seems radiant. An equally luminous pathos surrounds Dame Peggy Ashcroft's Barbie Batchelor, a sad little figure of baffled devotion." And Geraldine James is "unremittingly sensible" as Sarah Layton.

Art Malik as Hari Kumar and Susan Wooldridge as Daphne Manners.

Right: Barbie Batchelor (Dame Peggy Ashcroft) and Fabia Drake as Mabel Layton.

Below: Captain Ronald Merrick (Tim Pigott-Smith) and Sarah Layton (Geraldine James).

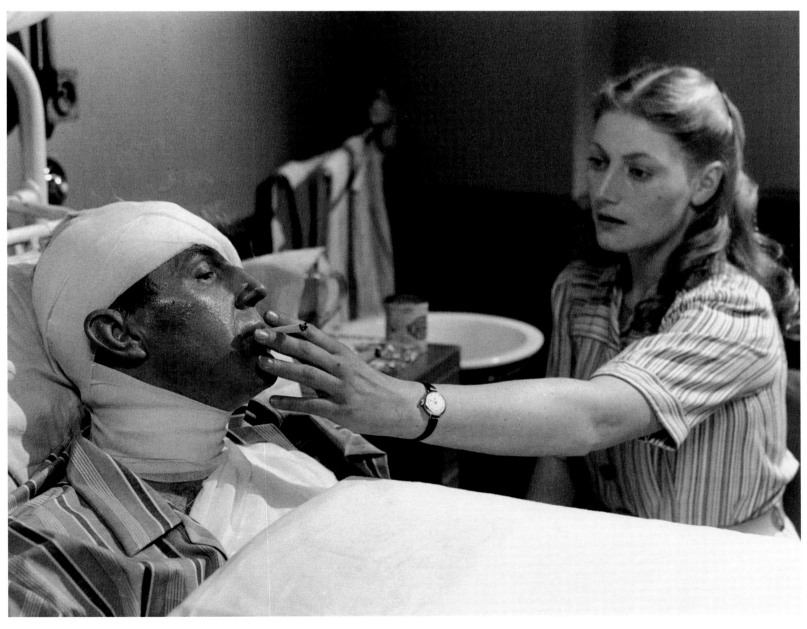

THE LAST PLACE ON EARTH
(6 episodes)

October 20 – November 24, 1985
Repeat: June 12 – July 17, 1988

Produced by: Central Independent
Television
Based on the book by Roland Huntford
Dramatized by: Trevor Griffiths
Producer: Tim Van Rellim
Director: Ferdinand Fairfax

Starring: Martin Shaw, Susan Wooldridge,
Sverre Anker Ousdal & Max Von Sydow

BLEAK HOUSE
(8 episodes)

December 1, 1985 – January 19, 1986

Produced by: BBC
Based on the novel by Charles Dickens
Dramatized by: Arthur Hopcraft
Producers: John Harris & Betty Willingale
Director: Ross Devenish

Starring: Diana Rigg, Denholm Elliott
& Suzanne Burden

LORD MOUNTBATTEN:
THE LAST VICEROY
(6 episodes)

January 26 – March 2, 1986
Repeat: May 1 – June 5, 1988

Produced by: George Walker Television
Productions
Based upon original scripts
Dramatized by: David Butler
Producer: Judith de Paul
Director: Tom Clegg
Music: John Scott

Starring: Nicol Williamson, Janet Suzman
& Ian Richardson

BY THE SWORD DIVIDED, Series I
(9 episodes)

March 23 – May 18, 1986

Produced by: BBC in association with
Consolidated Productions
Based upon original material
Dramatized by: John Hawkesworth,
Alexander Baron, Jeremy Paul
& Alfred Shaughnessy
Producer: Brian Spiby
Directors: Henry Herbert & Brian Farnham

Starring: Julian Glover, Sharon Mughan
& Rob Edwards

THE IRISH R.M., Series II
(6 episodes)

May 25 – June 29, 1986

Produced by: Little Bird in association with
Ulster Television and RTE
Based on the book by Somerville and Ross
Adapted by: Rosemary Anne Sisson
Producers: Christopher Neame &
James Mitchell
Directors: Peter Sykes & Roy Ward Baker

Starring: Peter Bowles & Bryan Murray

Mobil Masterpiece Theatre presents
Charles Dickens'

BLEAK HOUSE

Starring Diana Rigg & Denholm Elliott
An eight-part series
Sundays at 9 PM
Begins December 8 on Channel 13 PBS
Host: Alistair Cooke

Jarndyce vs. Jarndyce:
No man alive could understand it—
or settle it.

cc closed captioned for hearing impaired viewers
Bleak House is available in paperback from Bantam Books.

Mobil **15** MOBIL MASTERPIECE THEATRE 15TH ANNIVERSARY SEASON 1985/6

Bleak House

On the first page of *Bleak House*, Dickens' prose evokes his subject: "Fog everywhere. Fog up the river, where it flows among green aits and meadows; fog down the river, where it rolls defiled among the tiers of shipping and the waterside pollutions of a great (and dirty) city."

And on the second page: "And hard by Temple Bar, in Lincoln's Inn Hall, at the very heart of the fog, sits the Lord High Chancellor in his High Court of Chancery."

Dickens' target in *Bleak House* is the befogged legal system, as epitomized by the Chancery, a court of equity. Among its functions is protecting and settling the inheritances of fatherless children. But in *Bleak House*, Dickens describes an all-too-typical case – Jarndyce vs. Jarndyce – which drags on for years while the inheritance money is swallowed up by legal fees.

By the time he wrote *Bleak House*, Dickens was Britain's most popular novelist – and one of its most effective social reformers. In *Bleak House*, he was on familiar ground, for he had worked as a shorthand reporter in the law courts. And, as he writes in the novel, "The one great principle of English law is to make business for itself."

A consummate storyteller, Dickens laces his attack on the legal system with one of his most intricate plots. Reviewing the television adaptation of "Bleak House," John Leonard of *New York* magazine recounts that the three wards in Chancery – Esther, Richard, and Ada – "will be adopted by the wealthy, sensitive, and far-too-noble John Jarndyce (Denholm Elliott). Esther will find out who her mother is, and the pretty and vapid Ada will fall in love with Richard [who] will be consumed by grievance and greed. And Tulkinghorn (Peter Vaughan), the lawyer who is also a monster – if there are no monsters, this can't be Dickens – will contrive like Tiberius."

Harriet Van Horne of *Newsday* called the production "immaculate, a joy to watch." And Thomas Hoving wrote in *Connoisseur*: "I found it an unequivocal masterpiece, equal in quality, power, delicacy, and pure dramatic effect to some of the finest films ever made.

"Watching the eight episodes is like visiting a gallery of fabulous paintings, intricately linked yet able to stand on their own as individual works of art as striking as the caricatures of Daumier."

Denholm Elliott as John Jarndyce.

Right: Suzanne Burden as Esther and Ada Clare as Lucy.

Below: Diana Rigg and Robin Bailey as Lady & Lord Dedlock.

PARADISE POSTPONED
(11 *episodes*)

October 19 – December 28, 1986

Produced by: Euston Films for
Thames Television
Original story by: John Mortimer
Dramatized by: John Mortimer
Producer: Jacqueline Davis
Director: Alvin Rakoff
Music: Roger Webb

Starring: Paul Shelley, Jill Bennett,
Peter Egan, Michael Hordern,
David Threlfall & Colin Blakely

GOODBYE MR. CHIPS
(3 *episodes*)

January 4 – January 18, 1987
Repeat: August 7 – August 21, 1988

Produced by: BBC/MGM
Original novel by James Hilton
Dramatized by: Alexander Baron
Producer: Barry Letts
Director: Gareth Davies

Starring: Roy Marsden & Jill Meager

LOST EMPIRES
(7 *episodes*)

January 25 – March 8, 1987

Produced by: Granada Television
Based on the novel by J. B. Priestley
Dramatized by: Ian Curteis
Producer: June Howson
Director: Alan Grint

Starring: Colin Firth, Beatie Edney,
John Castle & Laurence Olivier

SILAS MARNER
(*Single* 2-*hour episode*)

March 15, 1987
Repeat: December 11, 1988

Produced by: BBC
Based on the novel by George Eliot
Dramatized by: Louis Marks &
Giles Foster
Producer: Louis Marks
Director: Giles Foster
Music: Carl Davis

Starring: Ben Kingsley, Patrick Ryecart
& Jenny Agutter

STAR QUALITY:
NOEL COWARD STORIES
(5 *episodes*)

March 29 – April 26, 1987

Produced by: BBC
Based on the short stories by Noel Coward
Producer: Alan Shallcross

"Star Quality"
Adapted by: Stanley Price
Director: Alan Dossor

Starring: Susannah York

"Mr. & Mrs. Edgehill"
Adapted by: T. R. Bowen
Director: Gavin Millar

Starring: Judi Dench

"Me & the Girls"
Adapted by: Ken Taylor
Director: Jack Gold

Starring: Tom Courtney

"Mrs. Capper's Birthday"
Adapted by: Jack Rosenthal
Director: Mike Ockrent

Starring: Patricia Hayes

"Bon Voyage"
Adapted by: Stanley Price
Director: Mike Vardy

Starring: Nigel Havers

THE DEATH OF THE HEART
(1 *episode*)

May 3, 1987

Produced by: Granada Television
Based on the novel by Elizabeth Bowen
Dramatized by: Derek Mahon
Producer: June Wyndham Davies
Director: Peter Hammond
Music: Geoffrey Burgon

Starring: Patricia Hodge, Nigel Havers,
Robert Hardy, Jojo Cole & Wendy Hiller

LOVE SONG
(2 *episodes*)

May 10 – May 17, 1987
Repeat: July 24 – July 31, 1988

Produced by: Anglia Television
Based on a short story by Jeffrey Archer
Dramatized by: Paul Ableman
Producer: John Rosenberg
Director: Rodney Bennett
Executive Producer: Sir John Woolf
Music: Dudley Simpson

Starring: Michael Kitchen,
Constance Cummings, Maurice Denham &
Diana Hardcastle

Silas Marner

At its best, an adapted classic can make us reexamine the book while it entertains us. George Eliot's *Silas Marner* is surely one such work.

For Americans now in middle age, *Silas Marner* is usually remembered as the one book they all had to read – at an age when the word "classic" was itself suspect.

When the BBC production appeared on Masterpiece Theatre in a single episode, Tom Shales of the *Washington Post* wrote: "The dust has been blown off the classic and the 'masterpiece' proves not only approachable but rewarding. As the child reawakens the old man's faith in life, so this production of 'Silas Marner' rekindles, for a bright two hours, a disillusioned old grump's belief in the salutary powers of television."

The "old man" is Silas Marner, a reclusive weaver who has spurned human contact since he was wrongly accused of theft and dismissed from his church. Settling in the village of Raveloe, he hoards his money, only to have it stolen from him. But he learns the redemptive power of love when a child arrives at his cottage after her mother falls dead in the snow.

After 15 years with the child, whom he names Eppie after his mother, Silas' happiness is threatened when her father seeks to reclaim her.

"The story remains gripping and surprisingly fresh in this time of headlines arising from child-custody battles," John O'Connor writes in the *New York Times*.

"The production beautifully captures the feel of a small village in the early 19th century.

"And the fine cast lends wonderful support to [Ben] Kingsley's intense and affecting portrait of a quiet, self-effacing man. There are no flashy pyrotechnics, only enormous and rewarding dedication."

Ben Kingsley as the reclusive weaver, Silas Marner.

Right and below: Elizabeth Hoyle plays Eppie, the child who animates Silas Marner's life.

THE BRETTS, Series I
(8 episodes)

October 11 – November 29, 1987

Produced by: Central Independent
Television
Original story by Rosemary Anne Sisson
Dramatized by: Rosemary Anne Sisson,
Laurence Marks, Maurice Gran, Bill Craig,
Julia Jones, Alan Clews, Stanley Price
& Freda Kelsall
Producer: Tony Charles
Director: Ronnie Wilson

Starring: Barbara Murray, Norman Rodway,
Belinda Lang, David Yelland,
George Winter, Rhoda Lewis, Janet Maw
& Patrick Hegarty

NORTHANGER ABBEY
(Single 90-minute episode)

December 6, 1987
Repeat: September 2, 1990

Produced by: BBC
Based on the novel by Jane Austen
Dramatized by: Maggie Wadey
Producer: Louis Marks
Director: Giles Foster
Music: Ilona Sekacz

Starring: Peter Firth, Robert Hardy,
Katharine Schlesinger & Googie Withers

SORRELL & SON
(5 episodes)

December 13 – January 10, 1988
Repeat: March 26 – April 23, 1989

Produced by: Yorkshire Television
Book by: Warwick Deeping
Dramatized by: Jeremy Paul
Producer: Derek Bennett
Director: Derek Bennett

Starring: Richard Pasco, Peter Chelsom
& Gwen Watford

FORTUNES OF WAR
(7 episodes)

January 17 – February 28, 1988
Repeat: July 23 – August 27, 1989

Produced by: BBC
Book by: Olivia Manning
Dramatized by: Alan Plater
Producer: Betty Willingale
Director: James Cellan Jones

Starring: Kenneth Branagh,
Emma Thompson, Ronald Pickup,
Charles Kay & James Villiers

THE DAY AFTER THE FAIR
(2 episodes)

March 6 – March 13, 1988
Repeat: August 19 – 26, 1990

Produced by: BBC
Based on Thomas Hardy's story,
On the Western Circuit
Dramatized by: Gillian Freeman
Producer: Louis Marks
Director: Anthony Simmons

Starring: Hannah Gordon, Anna Massey,
Sammi Davis & Martyn Stanbridge

DAVID COPPERFIELD
(5 episodes)

March 27 – April 24, 1988
Repeat: September 10 – October 8, 1989

Produced by: BBC
Book by: Charles Dickens
Dramatized by: James Andrew Hall
Producer: Terrance Dicks
Director: Barry Letts

Starring: Nolan Hemmings, Colin Hurley,
Brenda Bruce, Simon Callow,
Jeremy Brudenell & Nyree Dawn Porter

BY THE SWORD DIVIDED, Series II
(10 episodes)

August 28 – October 9, 1988

Produced by: BBC in association with
Consolidated Productions
Based on original material by
John Hawkesworth
Dramatized by: John Hawkesworth,
Alexander Baron & Jeremy Paul
Producer: Jonathan Allwyn
Director: Brian Farnham, Michael Custance
& Diarmuid Lawrence
Music: Ken Howard

Starring: Rob Edwards, Sharon Mughan,
Timothy Bentinck, Lucy Aston, Peter Birch
& Rosalie Crutchley

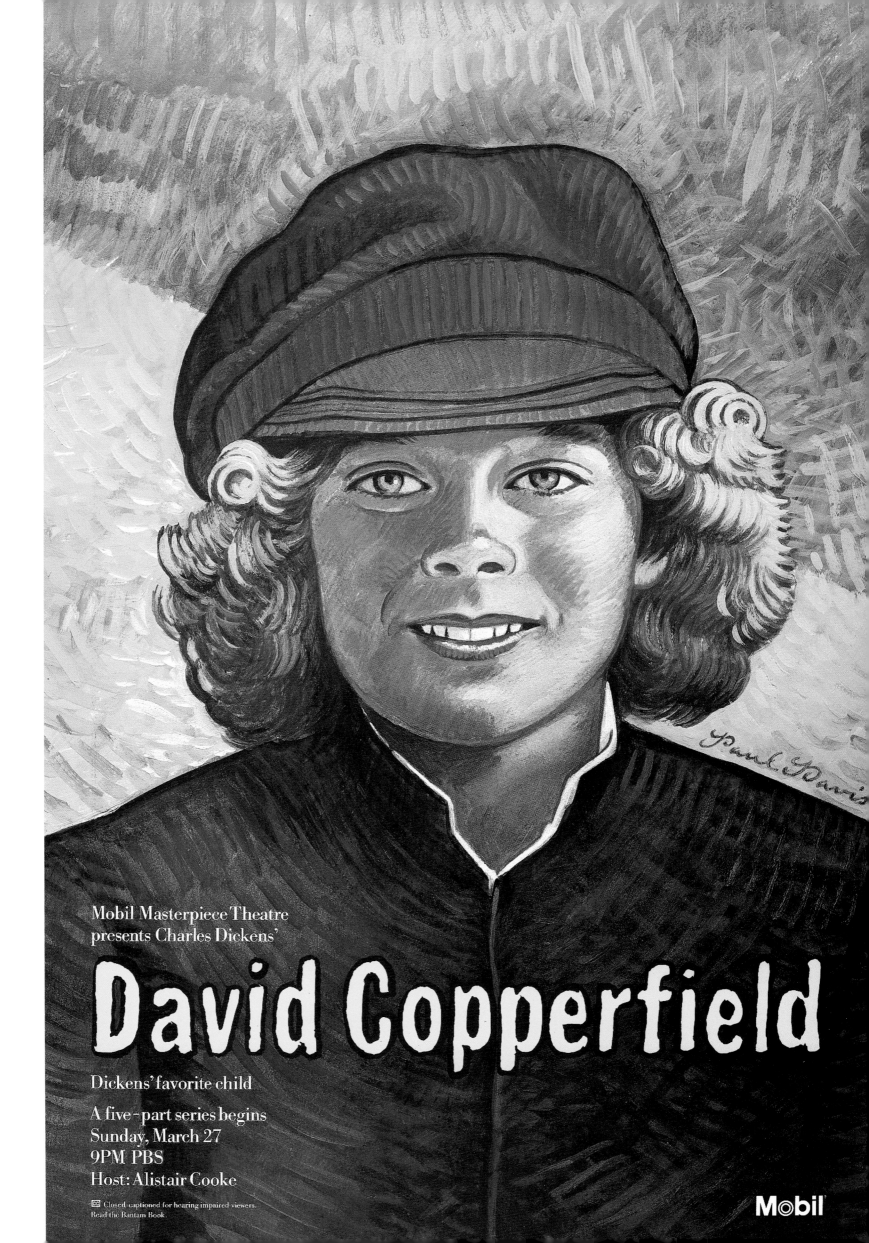

Mobil Masterpiece Theatre
presents Charles Dickens'

David Copperfield

Dickens' favorite child

A five-part series begins
Sunday, March 27
9PM PBS
Host: Alistair Cooke

Closed-captioned for hearing impaired viewers.
Read the Bantam Book.

Mobil

David Copperfield

"Originally written as a series, the novel is ideally constructed for television adaptation, for it moves from cliffhanger to cliffhanger with irresistible urgency," writes Margaret Drabble in *TV Guide*.

The work is Charles Dickens' *David Copperfield*, which he called "his favorite child" – not least because it closely resembles his own boyhood and youth. The hero, David Copperfield, survives an appalling childhood instigated by his father's death and his mother's remarriage. His stepfather, Murdstone, sends David away to a grim boarding school run by a sadistic headmaster, then to London to work in a rat-infested warehouse.

"The young Dickens had lived off bread and scraps of beef when he labelled bottles in a warehouse," says Alistair Cooke. "He too had known a shabby, genteel character like Micawber – his father, in fact – who had to go off with his family to a debtor's prison."

Until then, David had been living with the Micawbers. He is now homeless and decides to walk 50 miles to the house of his great-aunt Betsey Trotwood. He then begins a new life. He becomes educated, is apprenticed to a lawyer, and falls in love. After his first wife, Dora, dies in childbirth, he marries Agnes, who has long been devoted to him.

David Copperfield "is a story of success, triumph and forgiveness," writes Drabble. "The little orphan overcomes the ogres of cruelty and poverty and becomes rich, admired and loved through those Victorian virtues of Self-Help and Hard Work."

This Masterpiece Theatre presentation, writes Terry Atkinson in the *Los Angeles Times*, is "not only an undeniable classic but also a first-class treatment . . . exquisitely produced and directed . . . and superbly cast, acted and photographed."

Colin Hurley as David Copperfield (center), flanked by Neal Swettenham as Tommy Traddles and Jenny McCracken as Clara Peggotty.

Right: Young David (Nolan Hemmings), with his aunt Betsey (Brenda Bruce).

Below: David and his first love, Dora (Francesca Hall).

A PERFECT SPY
(7 episodes)

October 16 – November 27, 1988
Repeat: August 26 – October 7, 1990

Produced by: BBC
Based on the novel by John le Carré
Dramatized by: Arthur Hopcraft
Producer: Colin Rogers
Director: Peter Smith
Music: Michael Storey

Starring: Ray McAnally, Peter Egan,
Dame Peggy Ashcroft, Alan Howard,
Jane Booker & Benedict Taylor

HEAVEN ON EARTH
(Single 2-hour episode)

December 4, 1988

Produced by: Primedia Productions
Based upon original material
Dramatized by: Margaret Atwood
& Peter Pearson
Producers: Duane Howard & Nancy Botkin
Director: Allan Kroeker
Music: Loreena McKennitt

Starring: R. H. Thomson, Cedric Smith, Huw
Davies & Sian Leisa Davies

A WREATH OF ROSES
(Single 90-minute episode)

January 8, 1989

Produced by: Granada Television
Based on a short story by Elizabeth Taylor
Dramatized by: Peter Prince
Producer: Roy Roberts
Director: John Madden
Music: Stanley Myers

Starring: Joanna McCullum, Fabia Drake
& Trevor Eve

A VERY BRITISH COUP
(2 episodes)

January 15 – 16, 1989
Repeat: March 4 – March 11, 1990

Produced by: Skreba Films for Channel 4
Based on the novel by Chris Mullen
Dramatized by: Alan Plater
Producers: Ann Skinner & Sally Hibbin
Director: Mick Jackson
Music: John Keane

Starring: Ray McAnally, Alan MacNaughtan
& Keith Allen

1988/89
International Emmy Award: Best Drama:
A VERY BRITISH COUP

ALL PASSION SPENT
(4 episodes)

January 22 – February 5, 1989

Produced by: BBC
Based on the novel by Vita Sackville-West
Dramatized by: Peter Buckman
Producer: Colin Rogers
Director: Martyn Friend
Music: Nigel Hess

Starring: Wendy Hiller, Maurice Denham,
Phyllis Calvert, Faith Brook,
John Franklyn-Robbins & Harry Andrews

TALKING HEADS:
BED AMONG THE LENTILS
(Single episode)

February 12, 1989
Repeat: December 31, 1989

Produced by: BBC
Based on the original monologue by
Alan Bennett
Producer: Innes Lloyd
Director: Alan Bennett
Music: George Fenton

Starring: Dame Maggie Smith

CHRISTABEL
(4 episodes)

February 19 – March 12, 1989

Produced by: BBC
Based on the novel by Christabel Bielenberg
Dramatized by: Dennis Potter
Producer: Kenith Trodd
Director: Adrian Shergold
Music: Stanley Myers

Starring: Stephen Dillon, Elizabeth Hurley,
Geoffrey Palmer & Dennis Christopher

THE CHARMER
(6 episodes)

April 30 – June 4, 1989
Repeat: May 27 – July 1, 1990

Produced by: London Weekend Television
Based on the books by Patrick Hamilton
Dramatized by: Allan Prior
Producer: Philip Hinchcliffe
Director: Alan Gibson
Music: Richard Rodney Bennett

Starring: Nigel Havers, Rosemary Leach,
Bernard Hepton, Fiona Fullerton
& Judy Parfitt

THE BRETTS, Series II
(8 episodes)

June 11 – August 13, 1989

Produced by: Central Independent Television
Based upon original scripts
Producer: Tony Charles
Director: Ronnie Wilson, David Reynolds,
Bill Hays & John Bruce
Music: Cullen & Mackay

Starring: Belinda Lang, Norman Rodway,
Barbara Murray, David Yelland,
George Winter & Tim Wylton

Talking Heads: Bed Among the Lentils

Mrs. Vicar, they call her. It's as if she were just an appendage of her husband Geoffrey, the vicar, with no identity of her own.

She wonders "why the vicar's wife has to go to church at all. A barrister's wife doesn't have to go to court. An actor's wife doesn't have to go to every performance. Why do I always have to be on parade?"

She hates the tasks she must do: her cooking is abysmal and her flower arrangements resemble "walking sticks in an umbrella stand." But the ladies of Geoffrey's congregation – "the fan club" – are always ready to take over: "If you think squash is a competitive activity, try flower arranging."

While Geoffrey is off "blessing a steam engine," Mrs. Vicar is drinking sherry and being seduced in a storeroom – among the lentils – by an Indian shopkeeper. But for this tart, witty, lonely woman, life is not a bed of lentils.

As played by Dame Maggie Smith, Mrs. Vicar is the sole performer in "Talking Heads: Bed Among the Lentils." For 50 minutes, she addresses the camera in a riveting monologue.

You don't usually see monologues on Masterpiece Theatre. But Alan Bennett's "Bed Among the Lentils" isn't just a monologue – "it's a drama," wrote the critic in London's *Independent*. For "Maggie Smith [holds] 50 minutes effortlessly with no more props than a black cardigan and an unearthly acting talent."

Kay Gardella of the New York *Daily News* calls her performance "a brilliantly executed high-wire act." And Marvin Kitman writes in *Newsday*: "Smith, who hasn't been in a TV studio for 15 years, turns in a performance that is totally stunning."

Alan Bennett wrote the TV classic, "An Englishman Abroad," and performed on stage in "Beyond the Fringe" with Peter Cook, Jonathan Miller, and Dudley Moore.

Dame Maggie Smith as Mrs. Vicar.

Right and below: for this tart, lonely vicar's wife, the only diversions are flower arranging, sherry, and a bed among the lentils.

GLORY ENOUGH FOR ALL
(2 90-minute episodes)

November 5 – 12, 1990
Repeat: December 16 – 23, 1990

Produced by: Gemstone Productions/
Primedia Productions
Based on two books by Michael Bliss
Written by: Grahame Woods
Producer: Gordon Hinch
Director: Eric Till
Music: Louis Applebaum

Starring: R. H. Thomson, Robert Wisden,
Michael Zelniker, Heather Hess,
Martha Henry & John Woodvine

A TALE OF TWO CITIES
(4 episodes)

November 19 – December 10, 1989

Produced by: Granada Television/Dune and
Antenne II
Based on the novel by Charles Dickens
Adapted by: Arthur Hopcraft
Producer: Roy Roberts
Director: Philippe Monnier
Music: Serge Franklin

Starring: James Wilby, Serena Gordon,
Sir John Mills, Anna Massey, Xavier Deluc,
Kathie Kriegel & Jean-Pierre Aumont

THE YELLOW WALLPAPER
(Single 90-minute episode)

December 17, 1989

Produced by: BBC
Based on the short story by
Charlotte Perkins Gilman
Adapted by: Maggie Wadey
Producer: Sarah Curtis
Director: John Clive
Music: Carl Davis

Starring: Stephen Dillon, Julia Watson,
Dorothy Tutin & Carolyn Pickles

AFTER THE WAR
(8 episodes)

January 7 – February 25, 1990

Produced by: Granada Television
Based on original material by Frederic
Raphael
Producers: Michael Cox & Sita Williams
Directors: John Madden, John Glenister
& Nicholas Renton
Music: Stephen Oliver

Starring: Adrian Lukis, Robert Reynolds,
Serena Gordon, Anton Rodgers,
Clare Higgins, Susannah York
& Denis Quilley

THE REAL CHARLOTTE
(4 episodes)

March 25 – April 8, 1990

Produced by: Granada Television/
Gandon Productions
Based on the novel by Somerville and Ross
Adapted by: Bernard McLaverty
Producer: Niall McCarthy
Director: Tony Barry
Music: Paul Corbett

Starring: Patrick Bergin, Jeananne Crowley,
Joanna Roth, Robin Lermitte
& Jemma Redgrave

THE DRESSMAKER
(Single 2-hour episode)

April 15, 1990

Produced by: Freeway Films
and Ronald Shedlo Productions
Based on the novel by Beryl Bainbridge
Executive Producer: John McGrath
Screenplay by: John McGrath
Producer: Ronald Shedlo
Director: Jim O'Brien
Music: George Fenton

Starring: Joan Plowright, Billie Whitelaw, Peter
Postlethwaite, Jane Horrocks & Tim Ransom

TRAFFIK
(5 episodes)

April 22 – May 20, 1990

Produced by: Carnival Films for Channel 4
Based on original material by Simon Moore
Producer: Brian Eastman
Director: Alastair Reid
Music: Tim Souster & Fiachre Trench

Starring: Lindsay Duncan, Bill Paterson,
Jamal Shah, Talat Hussain, Tilo Prückner
& Fritz Müller-Scherz

1989/90
International Emmy Award: Best Drama:
TRAFFIK

PIECE OF CAKE
(6 episodes)

July 8 – August 12, 1990

Produced by: Holmes Associates with
London Weekend Television
Based on the novel by Derek Robinson
Adapted by: Leon Griffiths
Executive Producer: Linda Agran
Producer: Andrew Holmes
Director: Ian Toynton
Music: Peter Martin

Starring: Nathaniel Parker,
Jeremy Northam, Boyd Gaines,
Helena Michell, David Horovitch,
Richard Hope & Neil Dudgeon

AND A NIGHTINGALE SANG
(Single 90-minute episode)

October 15, 1989

Produced by: Portman Productions
Based on the play by C. P. Taylor
Dramatized by: Jack Rosenthal
Executive Producer: Victor Glynn
Producer: Philip Hinchcliffe
Director: Robert Knights

Starring: Joan Plowright, Phyllis Logan,
Tom Watt, John Woodvine, Pippa Hinchley
& Stephen Tompkinson

PRECIOUS BANE
(2 episodes)

October 22 – 29, 1989
Repeat: September 9 – 16, 1990

Produced by: BBC
Based on the novel by Mary Webb
Adapted by: Maggie Wadey
Producer: Louis Marks
Director: Christopher Menaul
Music: Rachel Portman

Starring: Janet McTeer, John McEnery,
John Bowe, Jim Carter & Clive Owen

CHARLES DICKENS'

A Tale of Two Cities

"The best of times... the worst of times" The epic story of romance and revolution.

A four-part series begins Sunday, November 19 9 P.M. on PBS Host: Alistair Cooke

Mobil®

Traffik

The scene is London, where a Tory Cabinet Minister vows to fight the flow of drugs into his country.

Cut to Hamburg, where a wealthy businessman runs an international heroin ring.

Cut to a poor opium grower in Pakistan.

These three stories interweave in "Traffik," winner of an International Emmy for best drama. While the story is fictional, the ramifications are real. "Traffik" is about those who grow, sell, capitalize on, and are addicted to heroin.

When confronted by the British minister, the Pakistani farmer denies his guilt: "I grow poppies," he says, "not heroin."

Since nothing but poppies will grow there, the farmer is victimized when the Pakistani government razes his fields.

For the minister, opium becomes more than a political issue when he learns that his daughter is a heroin addict.

And the jailing of the German magnate does nothing to stop the drug cartel, which is taken over by his wife.

In writing "Traffik," Simon Moore says: "I wanted to show the complete spectrum, how everything is connected – constructed from beginning to end."

Reviewing the series in *Mirabella*, Emily Prager writes that "Traffik" is "a brilliant fictional account of the complex tapestry that is the worldwide drug trade."

She adds: "'Traffik' is a thoroughly satisfying thriller, but it's also researched so well that anyone watching will come away with an understanding of the drug problem that far exceeds the cops-and-robbers scenario preferred by most Western governments."

Bill Paterson as Cabinet Minister Jack Lithgow and Feryal Gauhar Shah as Roomana.

Right: Jamal Shah plays Fazal, an opium grower in Pakistan.

Below: Ronan Vibert (Lee) and Julia Ormond (Caroline) are two heroin addicts in London.

THE HEAT OF THE DAY
(Single 2-hour episode)

September 30, 1990

Produced by: Granada Television
Based on the novel by Elizabeth Bowen
Adapted by: Harold Pinter
Producer: June Wyndham Davies
Director: Christopher Morahan

Starring: Patricia Hodge, Michael Gambon, Michael York & Dame Peggy Ashcroft

THE GINGER TREE
(4 episodes)

October 14 – November 4, 1990

Produced by: BBC and NHK
Based on the novel by Oswald Wynd
Adapted by: Christopher Hampton
Executive Producers: Alan Shallcross, Naonori Kawamura & Marilyn Hall
Producer: Tim Ironside-Wood
Directors: Morimasa Matsumoto & Anthony Garner
Music: Dominic Muldowney

Starring: Samantha Bond, Daisuke Rye, Fumi Dan & Joanna McCallum

JEEVES AND WOOSTER
(5 episodes)

November 11 – December 9, 1990

Produced by: Carnival Films for Granada Television
Based on the stories of P. G. Wodehouse
Dramatized by: Clive Exton
Executive Producer: Sally Head
Producer: Brian Eastman
Director: Robert Young

Starring: Hugh Laurie & Stephen Fry

SCOOP
(Single 2-hour episode)

December 30, 1990

Produced by: London Weekend Television
Based on the novel by Evelyn Waugh
Adapted by: William Boyd
Executive Producers: Nick Elliott & Patrick Garland
Producer: Sue Birtwistle
Director: Gavin Millar
Music: Stanley Myers

Starring: Michael Maloney, Nicola Pagett, Denholm Elliott, Michael Hordern, Herbert Lom, Donald Pleasence & Sverre Anker Ousdal

A ROOM OF ONE'S OWN
(Single episode)

January 6, 1991

Produced by: Oyster Television/ Thames Television
Based on lectures by Virginia Woolf
Adapted by: Patrick Garland
Producer: Bill Shepherd
Director: Patrick Garland

Starring: Eileen Atkins

TWENTIETH ANNIVERSARY FAVORITES
(9 episodes)

January 13 – March 10, 1991
All Repeat Episodes

UPSTAIRS/DOWNSTAIRS
"Guest of Honour"
"Such a Lovely Man"
"All the King's Horses"

THE FLAME TREES OF THIKA, Episode 3

ON APPROVAL

I, CLAUDIUS, Episode 9

ALL FOR LOVE: A DEDICATED MAN

ELIZABETH R, Episode 1

THE JEWEL IN THE CROWN, Episode 1

THE TALE OF BEATRIX POTTER

THE SIX WIVES OF HENRY VIII, Episode 5

HOUSE OF CARDS
(4 episodes)

March 31 – April 21, 1991

Produced by: BBC
Written by: Andrew Davies
Producer: Ken Riddington
Director: Paul Seed

Starring: Ian Richardson & Susannah Harker

SUMMER'S LEASE
(4 episodes)

May 12 – June 2, 1991

Produced by: BBC
Based on a novel by John Mortimer
Producer: Colin Rogers
Director: Martyn Friend
Music by: Nigel Hess

Starring: John Gielgud, Susan Fleetwood, Michael Pennington, Rosemary Leach, Mel Martin & Fyodor Chaliapin

MOBIL MASTERPIECE THEATRE PRESENTS
JOHN MORTIMER'S
SUMMER'S LEASE
STARRING
SIR JOHN GIELGUD

A FOUR-PART SERIES BEGINS SUNDAY, MAY 12 9 PM ON PBS HOST: ALISTAIR COOKE

The Heat of the Day

Stella and Robert are lovers joined in "that intimate and loose little society of the garrison" created by the German bombings of London in the early years of World War II.

"For Stella, her early knowing of Robert was associated with the icelike tinkle of broken glass being swept up among the crisping leaves, and with the charred freshness of every morning," Elizabeth Bowen writes in *The Heat of the Day*.

The intensity of their love – indeed, its very existence – is bound up with this time of peril. "They were the creatures of history, whose coming together was of a nature possible in no other way," Bowen writes.

Bowen's novel is bred of experience, for she was an air raid warden in London during the war. In her sensitive account of these days, writes Alistair Cooke, "no other novel about the Second War begins to touch *The Heat of the Day* for distilling the daily, and nightly, experience of living in London under siege."

Harold Pinter, who adapted the work for television, has emotional and artistic ties to the story. He too lived in London during the war, finding unexploded incendiary bombs in his back garden, before finally being evacuated from the city. Even more to the point, Pinter is a writer with an acute sense of the sinister undercurrents that run through Bowen's novel.

The plot, in fact, smacks of Pinter: Early in the work, an enigmatic stranger named Harrison tells Stella that Robert is selling secrets to the enemy. He offers to remain silent if Stella becomes his mistress.

Stella must now decide between learning the truth about Robert and protecting him. When she first confronts him, he denies Harrison's allegation. Only later does he admit that he has been a traitor, and condemns her ideas of patriotism and freedom: "Look at your free people – mice let loose in the middle of the Sahara . . . look at your mass of 'free' suckers, your democracy – kidded along from the cradle to the grave."

The television production stars Patricia Hodge (Stella) and Michael Gambon (Harrison), both of whom have appeared in several Pinter plays, as well as Michael York (Robert).

Michael Gambon as Harrison.

Right: Dame Peggy Ashcroft as Cousin Nettie.

Below: Stella (Patricia Hodge) with her lover Robert (Michael York), a Nazi collaborator.

Index

After the War, 104
All for Love, 84
All Passion Spent, 100
And a Nightingale Sang, 104
Anna Karenina, 46, 50-51
Barchester Chronicles, The, 84
Bleak House, 88, 90-91
Bretts, The, Series I, 96
Bretts, The, Series II, 100
By the Sword Divided, Series I, 88
By the Sword Divided, Series II, 96
Cakes and Ale, 38
Charmer, The, 100
Christabel, 100
Citadel, The, 80, 82-83
Clouds of Witness, 30
Cold Comfort Farm, 18
Country Matters, Series I, 34
Country Matters, Series II, 52
Cousin Bette, 24, 26-27
Crime and Punishment, 64, 66-67
Danger UXB, 64
David Copperfield, 96, 98-99
Day After the Fair, The, 96
Death of the Heart, The, 92
Dickens of London, 46
Disraeli: Portrait of a Romantic, 58, 60-61
Drake's Venture, 76
Dressmaker, The, 104
Duchess of Duke Street, The, Series I, 52
Duchess of Duke Street, The, Series II, 58
Edward and Mrs. Simpson, 70
Edwardians, The, 30
Elizabeth R, 19, 20-21
First Churchills, The, 18
Five Red Herrings, 42
Flame Trees of Thika, The, 70, 74-75
Flickers, 70
Fortunes of War, 96
Gambler, The, 18
Ginger Tree, The, 108
Glory Enough for All, 104
Golden Bowl, The, 24, 28-29
Good Soldier, The, 76
Goodbye Mr. Chips, 92
Heat of the Day, The, 108, 110-111
Heaven on Earth, 100
House of Cards, 108
How Green Was My Valley, 42
I, Claudius, 46, 48-49
I Remember Nelson, 70
Irish R.M., The, Series I, 80
Irish R.M., The, Series II, 88
Jeeves and Wooster, 108
Jewel in the Crown, The, 84, 86-87
Jude the Obscure, 18
Kean, 58
Last of the Mohicans, The, 19
Last Place on Earth, The, 88

Lillie, 52, 56-57
Little Farm, The, 30
Lord Mountbatten: The Last Viceroy, 88
Lost Empires, 92
Love for Lydia, 58, 62-63
Love in a Cold Climate, 70
Love Song, 92
Madame Bovary, 42, 44-45
Man Who Was Hunting Himself, The, 30
Mayor of Casterbridge, The, 52, 54-55
Moonstone, The, 24
Murder Must Advertise, 34
My Son, My Son, 58
Nancy Astor, 80
Nine Tailors, The, 34
Northanger Abbey, 96
Notorious Woman, 38
On Approval, 76
Our Mutual Friend, 46
Paradise Postponed, 92
Pere Goriot, 18
Perfect Spy, A, 100
Pictures, 80
Piece of Cake, 104
Point Counterpoint, 24
Poldark, I and II, 42
Possessed, The, 18
Precious Bane, 104
Pride and Prejudice, 64, 68-69
Private Schultz, 76
Real Charlotte, The, 104
Resurrection, 18
Room of One's Own, A, 108
Scoop, 108
Shoulder to Shoulder, 38, 40-41
Silas Marner, 92, 94-95
Six Wives of Henry VIII, The, 19, 22-23
Sons and Lovers, 76, 78-79
Sorrell & Son, 96
Spoils of Poynton, The, 18
Star Quality: Noel Coward Stories, 92
Strangers and Brothers, 84
Summer's Lease, 108
Sunset Song, 38
Tale of Beatrix Potter, The, 80
Tale of Two Cities, A, 104
Talking Heads: Bed Among the Lentils, 100, 102-103
Testament of Youth, 64
Thérèse Raquin, 64
To Serve Them All My Days, 76
Tom Brown's Schooldays, 24
Town Like Alice, A, 70, 72-73
Traffik, 104, 106-107
Twentieth Anniversary Favorites, 108
Unpleasantness at the Bellona Club, The, 30
Upstairs, Downstairs, Series I, 30, 32-33
Upstairs, Downstairs, Series II, 34, 36-37
Upstairs, Downstairs, Series III, 38
Upstairs, Downstairs, Series IV, 42
Vanity Fair, 24
Very British Coup, A, 100
Vienna 1900, 34
Winston Churchill – The Wilderness Years, 76
Wreath of Roses, A, 100
Yellow Wallpaper, The, 104